In Flanders Fields

—

In Flanders fields the poppies blow
Between the crosses, row on row
That mark our place;
The larks, still bravely su
Scarce heard amid the g

We are the Dead. Short [...] ago
We lived, felt dawn, saw sunset glow,
Loved, and were loved, and now we lie
In Flanders fields.

Take up our quarrel with the foe:
To you from failing hands we throw
The torch; be yours to hold it high.
If ye break faith with us who die
We shall not sleep, though poppies grow
In Flanders fields

John McCrae
—

Punch
Dec 8 · 1915

Major John McCrae (PAC C19919)

IN FLANDERS FIELDS
The Story of John McCrae

John F. Prescott

1985

THE BOSTON MILLS PRESS

CANADIAN CATALOGUING IN PUBLICATION

Prescott, John F. (John Francis), 1949-
   In Flanders Fields : the story of John McCrae

Bibliography: p.
ISBN 0-919783-07-4

1. McCrae, John, 1872-1918 - Biography. 2. Poets,
Canadian (English) - 20th century - Biography. *
3. Canada. Canadian Army - Biography. 4. Physicians - Canada - Biography. I. Title.

PS8525.C72Z86 1985   C811'.52   C85-098926-4
PR9199.2.M22Z86 1985

© John F. Prescott, 1985

Published by:
THE BOSTON MILLS PRESS
98 Main Street
Erin, Ontario N0B 1T0
(519) 833-2407

Design by John Denison
Typeset by Speed River Graphics
Printed by Ampersand, Guelph

Major funding for this volume was provided through the Ontario Heritage
Foundation, Ontario Ministry of Citizenship and Culture. We wish also to
acknowledge the financial assistance of The Canada Council, the Ontario
Arts Council and the Office of the Secretary of State.

ACKNOWLEDGEMENTS

I am grateful to many people for their help in producing this book. The seeds were sown by Charles Macauley, O.S.B., when he introduced a small boy to the poetry of Wilfred Owen. My father's discovery of the McCrae Birthplace Museum on a visit to Guelph got me started. The staff of the Osler Library in Montreal, Dr E.H. Bensley the Honorary Librarian, Dr Philip Teigen the Osler Librarian, and Miss M. Franciszyn were unfailingly helpful and enthusiastic, and have allowed me to quote from some of the manuscripts in their care. I thank the Directors of the John McCrae Birthplace Museum for allowing access to their museum; the Board of the Guelph Civic Museums and Ian Vincent, the Board's Curator, for permission to quote from material and reproduce photographs and sketches in the museum collection; Corey Broster, Curator of the McCrae Birthplace Museum. Mrs R. Gardner-Medwin, John McCrae's niece and the copyright holder of his unpublished writings, kindly allowed the quotations from the letters of John McCrae, many of which she has donated to the Public Archives of Canada. Mrs D.D. Campbell, John McCrae's other niece, helped by the loan of some books and in other ways. Others who allowed quotations from unpublished material were Mrs Cynthia Macleod, Dr H. Rock Robertson the Archivist of the Royal College of Physicians and Surgeons of Canada, and the Guelph Public Library.

The following allowed quotations from published material: Mrs D.M. Lindsay (Sir Andrew Macphail's daughter), Dr R. Palmer Howard, Fitzhenry and Whiteside Ltd., Geographia Ltd., and Messrs. Hodder and Stoughton Ltd. Mrs Cynthia Macleod kindly provided the photograph of her father (C.L.C. Allinson), and Dr R. Palmer Howard that of Thomas McCrae and Sir William Osler. Other photographs came from the McCrae Birthplace Museum (Guelph Museums) and the Public Archives of Canada. Joel Duncan and Richard Johnston copied the Guelph photographs.

Others who helped were Eric Elstone, Elsie Low, Peter Hohenadel, Jeremy Prescott, and the late Verne McIlwraith. I am grateful to Dr Curtis Fahey for editing the book and for his comments, and to John Denison, publisher of the Boston Mills Press, for his enthusiasm. The Ontario Ministry of Citizenship and Culture provided a grant towards the cost of editing and printing the book, for which I am most grateful.

Finally, this book could not have been written without the help and encouragement of Cathy Prescott, to whom it is dedicated.

Canadian Stretcher Bearers bringing wounded through the mud. Battle of Passchendaele, November 1917. (Public Archives of Canada, PA 2367)

PREFACE

This book is a study of John McCrae, author of the most popular poem of the First World War, *In Flanders Fields*. The poem made the poppy a symbol inseparable from the war and is used every Remembrance Day throughout the countries of the old British Empire. The book is the story of how the poem came to be written and of its reception, but mainly it is the story of an exceptionally gifted and cultured man who would have been well known even had he not written the poem.

My interest in McCrae followed arrival in the town of his birth — Guelph, Ontario — where there is a small museum in his honour. As a boy I had known old men in England who vividly described the horrors of their Great War, and their bitterness at its waste. At school I had been moved by the poems of the remarkable English poets of the war — Siegfried Sassoon, Herbert Read, Edmund Blunden, but above all Wifred Owen. Reared on these poets it was hard to understand how a Canadian physician, well acquainted with war, could have written such a bloodthirsty little poem. This book tells the story, and now I understand.

If the poem had been McCrae's only contribution then the story would hardly have been worth telling. But as I learned more about the man the story became more fascinating because his life was of such vigour, and yet of sensitivity, and the years in which he lived were ones of great change. It is thus also the story of the resilience of the Scottish pioneers and of their descendants in Canada, of the revolution in medicine, of the imperial period of Canadian life, of the heroism and sacrifice of Canadians in the Great War, and of the transition of Canada from a colony to a nation. Men of McCrae's quality are seldom met or made, but though his laughter echoes down the years the full story is the tragedy of a good man affected deeply by war.

To some extent this book is a contribution to my adopted country in gratitude for the happy years I have had here — it was a good way to learn some Canadian history. I hope that the future of Canada can be guided by some of the spirit and truth-seeking of McCrae. The book is a reminder, of which there cannot be enough, that militarism and war are not answers to the dilemmas of the human condition. Nations have to beat their swords into ploughshares.

John Prescott
Guelph, 1985

John McCrae with his mother, brother Tom, and sister Geills.
(McCrae Birthplace Museum)

CHAPTER ONE
EARLY LIFE: 1872-87

John McCrae was born on 30 November, 1872 in a small stone cottage in Guelph, Ontario, the second son of David McCrae and his wife, Janet. The McCraes were Scottish Presbyterians with the resilience and self-reliance of second-generation pioneers in Canada, and with the strong traditions of a Scottish clan. In the 17th century McCraes had supported the Episcopal Church and the House of Stuart, and some had later fought against the English in the rebellions of 1715 and 1745. Following the 1745 rebellion in Scotland, the choices open to the supporters of that revolt were emigration or military service; service in the English army became a McCrae tradition. McCraes served the Hanoverian kings of England with distinction in the wars in India and Europe. McCraes are also recorded over the centuries as talented physicians or surgeons. Skill in Gaelic poetry was yet another tradition in the McCrae clan.

John's great grandfather, David McCrae, was born in Scotland in 1800. He married Marion Munroe and they had five children, of whom the eldest was Thomas, John's grandfather. Thomas married Jean Campbell, the daughter of an Ayrshire farmer and a descendant of Scottish Covenanters. The Campbell family was proud of its descent from Covenanters, men and women prepared to die for their beliefs.

In 1849 Thomas McCrae emigrated with his family to Canada and settled in Guelph, where he obtained work as a book-keeper. By 1853 he was in a lumber business and had purchased timber rights in East Flamborough, about 20 miles from Guelph. Thompson, McCrae & Company erected a water-powered saw-mill on a 200 acre section in East Flamborough which continued in operation until the timber was exhausted. In 1859 McCrae bought out Thompson and a few years later was engaged in woollen-weaving under the name of Armstrong, McCrae and Company, a firm later to become the Guelph Woollen Mills when McCrae bought out Armstrong. The business grew rapidly during the American Civil War, and in 1867 a large factory was built. By 1885 McCrae and Company was employing 250 people, but later the firm went into a decline associated with the poor economy of later nineteenth-century Canada.

In 1863 Thomas bought Janefield, a farm on the edge of Guelph. He became a noted breeder of cattle, sheep, and horses. Active as an elder in the Presbyterian church, he was a Liberal in politics. Among his other offices were justice of the peace, chairman of the Board of Health, and superintendent of the Sunday school. He was an ardent patriot: at the time of the *Trent* affair during the American Civil War he volunteered 15 teams of horses for the anticipated fight with the United States.

John McCrae's father, David, was four when the family emigrated to Canada. He was educated in Guelph and in 1862 enrolled in the first course offered by the newly founded Ontario Veterinary College. Despite a year of training, on graduation he worked briefly for his father before joining the army. After his father's death, he became, at the age of 33, manager of the Guelph Woollen Mill and owner of Janefield. David subsequently sold the mills to pay off the mortgage on them; farming and soldiering were more attractive to him than commerce.

Like his father, David was to become a prize-winning breeder of Galloway cattle. He was active in farming and journalism, and was partly responsible for the founding of what became the Ontario Agricultural College. Also, like his father, he was a Liberal, an elder of St. Andrew's Presbyterian Church, and superintendent of the Sunday school. His journals speak of regular church attendance, recording always the text and sermon for the day. His main source of income in later years was as a director of the North American Life Insurance Company. The family was not wealthy partly because David, seeking to regain the fortune lost with the sale of the mills, seems to have made unproductive speculations in farmland, but principally because of his prolonged association with the army.

David McCrae's first joy was soldiering. At the age of 20 he was commissioned in the 47th Foot but later transferred to the 16th Foot as a 1st Lieutenant, returning in 1866 to Guelph to join the local militia, the Wellington Rifles. That year, in response to the Fenian raids from the United States, he organized the Guelph Company of the Wellington Rifles into a garrison battery of artillery. David served until the end of the raids and then organized the Wellington Field Battery, the successor to the garrison battery. He left the militia to serve for a number of years as a regular officer at artillery headquarters. Resigning from the regular army in 1879, he became commanding officer of a militia unit in Guelph, the 1st Brigade of Field Artillery. His love of soldiering continued into old age. In 1915, at the age of 70, he recruited the 43rd Battery. He took his men to England in 1916 but was not allowed to go to France with them.

John McCrae's mother, Janet, was the daughter of John Eckford, a Presbyterian minister in Scotland and later a pioneer and school superintendent in Canada. As a young man he had wanted to join the 42nd Highlanders, the Black Watch. His pride in the exploits of Scottish regiments was to remain strong but, being an elder son, he chose the ministry. His wife died of typhoid in 1847, and in 1850 he resigned from the ministry and emigrated to Canada with his three children. Unable to obtain passage on their booked ship, the *Wolfville*, they were detained in poverty in Glasgow to await the next boat, the *Clutha*. At Quebec they saw the *Wolfville* anchored in the St Lawrence and flying the yellow flag of quarantine; cholera had broken out. The Eckfords felt that they had been preserved for some special destiny.

John Eckford bought land in the forests of Walkerton and Brant. Their early life was difficult; they arrived at their shanty in bitter cold and snow six feet deep. It snowed daily for three months and the tree stumps from that winter's choppings were two feet higher than those of an ordinary season. The Eckford's first wheat harvest was a pathetic, but thrilling, 24 shocks of wheat, flailed by hand and winnowed on the wind.

Janet Eckford was a voracious reader, who was taught by her father to read Greek and Latin by the light of the fire. She loved books all her life, in part because they were an escape from the hardships of pioneer life, but also because they were part of the Presbyterian tradition of plain living and high thinking. John Eckford's legacy to his daughter Janet was cheerfulness in service to others, a religious faith nurtured by the hardships of his life, and a cultured intellect. These qualities and the self-reliance and endurance of the pioneers were her gifts to the three children of her marriage in 1870 to David McCrae — Thomas, John, and Geills. David's legacy to his children was a fighting spirit, pride in the achievements of the family's forebears, and the strong faith of his ancestors.

Guelph was first settled in 1827. The city developed rapidly as a result of the growth of agriculture in Wellington County. By 1872, when John McCrae was born, the city's population was about 9,000.

At the age of 12, John went to the Guelph Collegiate Institute, where he studied English under William Tytler. He acquired from Tytler a love for writing and for poetry which, like soldiering, lasted throughout his life. Holidays were spent at his grandfather's but in later adolescent years he suffered from asthma and would sleep in the house of Dr. Howitt, the local physician and a family friend, rather than on the family farm. He was influenced by both his parents in his religion and in his love of the military.

John's father encouraged his interest in the military with stirring stories of British victories, saying that "one Englishman equals three Frenchmen." John, like most of his generation, read the English *Boys Own Paper*, in whose view British boyhood should be spent in active preparation for imperial and military glory. His involvement with the military started young; at 14 he joined the Highland Cadet Corps in the school, which was organized by a veteran of the Crimean War who taught bayonet drill and marching. John was always proud of his association with the corps. He won the gold medal offered by the Minister of Education for the best drilled cadet in Ontario. At 15 he became a bugler in his father's battery and enrolled as a gunner when he was 18. In 1888, at the age of 16, he matriculated to the University of Toronto, the first pupil of the Guelph Collegiate Institute to win a scholarship to that institution.

John learned by heart the *Shorter Catechism* of the Presbyterian Church before he could read and acquired early a religious frame of mind. He was to become an indefatigable churchgoer. Raised in the Presbyterian tradition, John had a strong sense of divine calling, a sense that he did everything to serve God, and he felt a responsibility for using his talents and gifts for the benefit of others. His early lessons bit deep, and there remained with him always an awareness of life's transience and a fervent commitment to duty.

*John McCrae (second row, on left) with fellow artillery officers on Militia
exercises, 1893. (McCrae Birthplace Museum)*

CHAPTER TWO
EARLY UNIVERSITY DAYS: 1888-93

Upon enrolling at the University of Toronto, John began studying for the Bachelor of Arts. He was a member of Knox College, the Presbyterian college to which his brother Tom also belonged. In his first year he attended 24 lectures a week in subjects that included German, Greek, Latin, French, Hebrew, English, and Biology. He worked hard and also attended church regularly, occasionally three times on Sundays, and missionary meetings when they occurred. His letters were at times critical of the preachers; following Presbyterian tradition, sermons were discussed and criticized at home since the Devil might cunningly use even the preacher as his mouthpiece. Throughout his days in Toronto he continued to be troubled by asthma, which was exacerbated by the city's polluted air. Sometimes he was sufficiently well to play rugby for the second university team with his brother. He performed with the Glee Club, giving one performance at the Toronto Lunatic Asylum where, he wrote, "the audience was not disposed to be particularly critical."

There is a story that John was going to become a Presbyterian minister, influenced by his family background and by the minister of St Andrews in Guelph. However, he was encouraged to study biology by Professor Ramsay Wright, and in his second and third years he studied the sciences, achieving the highest mark in the second year and second place in the third year. Illness prevented his reaching the top place.

At Toronto, John continued his interest in soldiering. He retained links with the Number 2 Battery in Guelph, becoming gunner in 1890, Quarter-Master Sergeant in 1891, and 2nd Lieutenant in 1893. In 1896 he became Lieutenant. At the university he was a member of "K" (Varsity) Company, the Queen's Own Rifles of Canada, a militia regiment in which he rose to be company captain. According to a fellow member and friend, Stephen Leacock, the company disintegrated through lack of support, being "often compelled to form imaginary fours with three in line." John was also a member of the Zeta Psi fraternity.

A friend, H.O. Howitt, later remembered John during his university days:

I like to think of Jack McCrae as he was when he lived in my father's house; tall, boyish, hair inclined to be wavy and fair; striking, sparkling eyes; teeth with hardly a filling in them, hard and a pearly colour, the second incisors slightly tilted; all of which, strange to say, added to his attractiveness and the infection of his smile. His smile was one of his greatest assets. His cheeks were inclined to be reddish; his head was well-formed; he had an excellent forehead. His expression changed frequently, but I think that when smiling he was most attractive. He wore clothing that was not generally considered fashionable — generally rough grey with considerable black mixed with it. His coats were shorter than the average person wore. They were not particularly well-tailored and seldom were his trousers pressed. I cannot remember him ever wearing other than black high shoes when in town. He never wore any jewellery, unless one could consider his silver watch-chain and the silver seal that dangled from it. His watch was also silver, and if I remember correctly, it was a hunting case and wound with a key. He often wore a polka-dot necktie; generally his collar was of a winged type. A number of his poems were written while he sat in the bay window at the front of my house.[1]

McCrae did indeed wear his clothes too tight. One story says that when McCrae was in London in 1904 he had himself measured by a tailor and for years thereafter he reordered his suits using these same measurements. The characteristic of wearing clothes too small was shared by his brother Tom, giving them "a curious familial, sartorial manner — Lady Osler, devoted to Tom, used to rail at both him and Jack for the shortness of their coats, and the obviousness of their gluteal expanse."[2] A girl who knew John well said: "He is so nice but ... why does he always insist on wearing clothes 6 sizes too small for him?"[3]

McCrae's university days were marred by asthma, which was so serious that after the third year he left Toronto for a year, to teach as assistant resident master at the Ontario Agricultural College in Guelph. During this year he became embroiled in a disgraceful episode in the college's history, becoming a pawn in a college power struggle and in Ontario politics.

The Ontario Agricultural College was founded in 1874 by the Ontario Government, which recognised that science would change the old pioneer farming methods. The large Ontario farming community showed some resentment towards the new institution, feeling that the success of farmers owed nothing to a college education, and the farmers generally thought the College a waste of taxpayers' money. This unhappy state of affairs was compounded by appointments to the staff based on political patronage rather than on merit; there was also a high turnover of staff based on low salaries.

As if all this were not enough, there was an administrative division within the college between the "inside department" where the pupils were taught theory, and the farm, the "outside department," where the students spent three to five hours a day in practical work. The farm superintendent, Thomas Shaw, detested the president, James Mills, and their quarreling led to disharmony in the faculty. There were also "scandals." In 1892 a teacher called E.L. Hunt, forced to resign as assistant resident and mathematical master after ten years in the post, went on to Knox College with a view to becoming a Presbyterian minister. This was a surprising ambition since he had been seen leaving the matron's room at three in the morning, having at other times been seen sitting on her knee.

It was hard to attract good students to the college, and some of the farmers' sons seem to have been louts who baited the faculty, complained about the food, and on occasion put pigs in the matron's room and stole the president's beer. Petitions to the Minister of Agriculture were endemic concerning the food, and in 1889 the graduating class had complained to the minister about Hunt's teaching. McCrae joined this unhappy college in the fall of 1892 as assistant resident master, teaching English and mathematics.

The trouble at the college was the failure of James Mills to control Thomas Shaw, a strong-willed and energetic man who had great influence among the students but few faculty supporters. One such supporter, Sharman, had gone to President Mills after Hunt's resignation and asked for the job of assistant resident master. Mills made it clear that he would instead be offered the more desirable professorship of agriculture. In all probability McCrae got the job of assistant resident master through his father's influence at both the college and with the Minister of Agriculture. David McCrae staunchly supported the artillery Battery on the campus. Mills, for his part, had little control of appointments to his staff. Sharman, a graduate of the college, was not made professor of agriculture and strongly resented McCrae's appointment.

At this stage McCrae was not a good teacher. His students were his own age or older, and English and mathematics did not interest some of the boys. A student, Newman, began a campaign against McCrae, saying that it was possible to ask questions he could not answer. He persuaded the third-year students not to take lectures from McCrae and raised a petition to Mills to have the teacher removed. Newman was encouraged in these activities by Shaw, who sometimes slighted McCrae to the students, and by Sharman. McCrae was unpopular with the students, though with the more loutish rather than with the more intelligent — "the class of student objecting to McCrae was very different to those who objected to Mr. Hunt."[4]

Matters came to a head when McCrae was thrown into a pond. Five students went to Toronto to meet the Premier of Ontario and asked for McCrae's dismissal because he showed an "inability to teach, ignorance of the subject taught, and negligence in preparing for his work," although he was a "good man to have in connection with the Battery." The Premier told the students that, in order to facilitate an investigation, they should return to their classes with McCrae. On the students resuming their classes Professor Shaw told them that they were making a great mistake and had lost an opportunity in returning without obtaining McCrae's dismissal. The government then appointed a commission of inquiry into the Ontario Agricultural College and Experimental Farm.

Meanwhile, shortly after the students' meeting with the Minister of Agriculture, David McCrae met with him as well. The students learned that the minister said that he would "stand by Jack thro' thick and thin." David McCrae accused Sharman and Shaw of being at the bottom of the whole episode and said that, if his son were forced to leave the college, two more would go with him. He charged Sharman publicly with wanting John's job and with stirring up the students. He told the students that "if my son cannot do the work he will have to go, but he must have justice."

The commission of inquiry found that Hunt was bitter towards the president because of the affair of the matron, and had agitated against him; Sharman was found to have interested himself unduly in the student campaign against McCrae, and the student Newman "evaded the questions in a very dishonest manner"; Shaw, it was concluded, had "systematically poisoned the minds of the students" in his power struggle with President Mills. Sharman, Newman, and Shaw left the college and McCrae resigned in October 1983 to complete the final year of his B.A. at the University of Toronbto. In 1897 he returned briefly to the college from the Toronto General Hospital to teach zoology.

The whole episode was deeply disturbing to a sensitive boy of 20. He was not then a good teacher, though later he was excellent. His writing and poetry of the period reveal a pedantic and overly sensitive boy who was ill-equipped to deal with the problems he encountered. The episode left him with a dislike of political factions. The reaction of his father in fighting injustice was typical of the direct approach of the McCraes and was one John emulated in later life.

During his time at the college McCrae had also fallen in love with the eighteen-year-old sister of a friend. The girl died of an infection during the year. The shock of her death was reflected in the poetry he wrote in the next few years.

CHAPTER THREE
MEDICAL STUDIES AND EARLY POETRY:
1894-98

McCrae returned to Toronto in late 1893 to complete his degree in Natural Sciences. He obtained his B.A. in 1894. For the last year of his B.A. and the first two years of his medical studies he was a fellow in biology under the supervision of Professor R. Ramsay Wright, a zoologist who in 1890 had been sent from Toronto to Berlin to study Koch's claim for a cure for tuberculosis. His brother Thomas McCrae had previously spent two years as a fellow with Wright.

John McCrae did outstandingly in his undergraduate work in biology and spent the summer of 1894 at Wood's Hole in Massachusetts in further study. He was strongly attracted to graduate work in zoology and thought of studying for a doctoral thesis in Edinburgh. Many, however, advised him that he should obtain a medical degree before deciding to do biological research, suggesting that, if such research proved unattractive or hard to make a living at, he could always fall back on medicine for a career.

McCrae studied medicine from 1894 to 1898. He was a dedicated student and won the gold medal in his graduating class. McCrae paid his own way through medical school, in part by tutoring, which was a privilege of being a fellow in biology. Two of his pupils were to become the first women physicians in Ontario; women were not allowed to study medicine formally at that time. During his holidays he worked as an assistant to Dr Howitt in Guelph, revisiting patients whom the busy doctor had previously seen. There was no shortage of work with typhoid common and with scarlet fever and diptheria endemic.

By taking practical anatomy, anatomy, and materia medica, McCrae was able to enrol in the second year of the four-year course. In the medical class there were about 20 men; in the Faculty of Medicine as a whole there were only 24. The 1891 prospectus reads like a circus broadsheet, promising that "facilities for clinical instruction have been immensely improved. Arrangements for instruction in Anatomy are now unsurpassed. The Faculty have spared no expense in making the arrangements for medical instruction perfect...." In surgery the prospectus promised that consideration would be given to "the part played by minute vegetative fungi, involving a consideration of the germ theory of disease."

In the 1890s a number of Toronto's outstanding medical graduates were sent by the professor of clinical medicine, J.E. Graham, to study with his friend William Osler at the Johns Hopkins Hospital in Baltimore. Some went to be resident physicians at the Garrett Hospital in Mount Airy, a summer convalescent home for the sick children of Baltimore; McCrae was sent there in the summer of his third year of medical studies. McCrae recorded his impressions in *The comedy of a hospital* published in *The Westminster*, a Presbyterian weekly. He wrote of the sayings and doings of the children, and of a black porter "raised in slavery (and in so far, good, a Southerner will tell you)," but also of the tragedy. From Mount Airy he wrote:

> A kitten has taken up with a poor cripple dying of muscular atrophy who cannot move. It stays with him all the time, and sleeps most of the day in his straw hat. Tonight I saw the kitten curled up under the bedclothes. It seems as it were a gift of Providence that the little creature should attach itself to the child who needs it most.

And of another child:

> The day she died she called for me all day, deposed the nurse who was sitting by her, and asked me to remain with her. She had to be held up on account of lack of breath and I had a tiring hour of it before she died, but it seemed to make her happier and was no great sacrifice. Her friends arrived twenty minutes too late. It seems hard that Death will not wait the poor fraction of an hour, but so it is.

McCrae published more poems during his days as a medical student than in his later years. He also published a few short stories of little interest in the student newspaper *Varsity* but also some in national magazines such as *Saturday Night* and *Godey's*. In 1898 he wrote a short study entitled *A modern soldier of fortune* in a book about Alexander Gardner published by Blackwoods in Edinburgh. It was a well-written story about the extraordinary exploits and misadventures of a Scottish mercenary in Afghanistan and the Punjab.

McCrae's poems written during these student days show the turmoil created by the tragic outcome of his love affair. They also show his sense both of religion and of the vanity of human aspiration; most conclude with death and its peace. The devastating effect of his love affair is described in the poem *Unsolved*. This feeling of guilt reflects the struggle between his idea of duty and service to God, and of God as he actually found him in a woman's eyes. *A song of comfort* displays acceptance of his tragedy.

Unsolved

Amid my books I lived the hurrying years,
    Disdaining kinship with my fellow man;
Alike to me were human smiles and tears,
    I cared not whither Earth's great life-stream ran,
Till as I knelt before my mouldered shrine,
    God made me look into a woman's eyes;
And I, who thought all earthly wisdom mine,
    Knew in a moment that the eternal skies

Were measured but in inches, to the quest
　　That lay before me in that mystic gaze.
"Surely I have been errant: it is best
　　That I should tread, with men their human ways."
God took the teacher, ere the task was learned,
And to my lonely books again I turned.

Canadian Magazine, 1895

The hope of my heart

I left, to earth, a little maiden fair,
　　With locks of gold, and eyes that shamed the light;
I prayed that God might have her in His care
　　　　And sight.

Earth's love was false; her voice, a siren's song;
　　(Sweet mother-earth was but a lying name)
The path she showed was but the path of wrong
　　　　And shame.

"Cast her not out!" I cry. God's kind words come —
　　"Her future is with Me, as was her past;
It shall be My good will to bring her home
　　　　At last."

Varsity, 1894

A song of comfort

　　　　　　Sleep, weary ones, while ye may —
　　　　　　　Sleep, oh, sleep!"
　　　　　　　　Eugene Field

Thro' May time blossoms, with whisper low,
The soft wind sang to the dead below:
"Think not with regret on the Springtime's song
And the task ye left while your hands were strong.
The song would have ceased when the Spring was past,
And the task that was joyous be weary at last."

To the winter sky when the nights were long
The tree-tops tossed with a ceaseless song:

"Do ye think with regret on sunny days
And the path ye left, with its untrod ways?
The sun might sink in a storm cloud's frown
And the path grow rough when the night came down."

In the grey twilight of the autumn eves,
It sighed as it sank through the dying leaves:
"Ye think with regret that the world was bright,
That your path was short and your task was light;
The path, though short, was perhaps the best
And the toil was sweet, that it led to rest."

Varsity, 1894

Other poems of this period are concerned with religion and death. The focus is on the meaning of life to McCrae, the poems reflecting a struggle between the traditional Christianity which he learned at home and the world as he actually found it. His love affair had awakened him to what the "world" offered, which conflicted with his Calvinist upbringing. What was the meaning of Christianity in the modern world? Was it believable or of any value? The poems show the fierce struggle which occurred between his understanding of Christianity and the attractions of love, materialism, and worldly pleasures. Clearly, and surprisingly for a hard-working student like McCrae, his love affair showed that life involved more than just work. And yet work was important and part of his family's tradition — though labour and good works could not buy a place in heaven; that depended on predestination, as described in *In due season.*

In due season

If night should come and find me at my toil,
    When all Life's day I had, tho' faintly, wrought,
And shallow furrows, cleft in stony soil
    Were all my labour: Shall I count it naught

If only one poor gleaner, weak of hand,
    Shall pick a scanty sheaf where I have sown?
"Nay, for of thee the Master doth demand
    Thy work: the harvest rests with Him alone."

The Westminster, 1897

In the end McCrae concluded that he was not able to judge the ways of God and that the world judged in a different way from the Creator. His place as a Christian was that of "humble toil with cheery face," to sow and not necessarily to reap, to follow the ways of Christ and leave the rest to God. The

20

poems McCrae wrote during these years are a summary of his faith, which was characterized by a rejection of materialism and by an acceptance of, and belief in, what he knew as God. He never seems to have questioned Christianity; still, the Toronto verses show the traditional inner struggle of many Christians over the meaning of their faith. For McCrae the end of this struggle was followed by the sense of peace portrayed in *Eventide*.

Eventide

The day is past and the toilers cease;
The land grows dim 'mid the shadows grey,
And hearts are glad, for the dark brings peace
       At the close of day.

Each weary toiler, with lingering pace,
As he homeward turns, with the long day done,
Looks out to the west, with the light on his face
       Of the setting sun.

Yet some see not (with their sin-dimmed eyes)
The promise of rest in the fading light;
But the clouds loom dark in the angry skies
       At the fall of night.

And some see only a golden sky
Where the elms their welcoming arms stretch wide
To the calling rooks, as they homeward fly
       At the eventide.

It speaks of peace that comes after strife,
Of the rest He sends to the hearts He tried,
Of the calm that follows the stormiest life —
       God's eventide.

Canadian Magazine, 1985

Many of the poems written in McCrae's early manhood, and some written after 1900, have a preoccupation with death. The achievement of peace after death was a constant theme in his poetry. He saw life as a struggle, both emotional and physical, and felt that only death would end the struggle — there was to be no rest in this world for the man reared in the Calvinist tradition. The asthma which dogged him for so much of his life was symptomatic of this struggle. During his asthmatic attacks he must have longed for oblivion — perhaps this was one reason why death was so often a theme in his poetry.

With his staunch Presbyterian upbringing McCrae kept his eye fixed firmly on the "chief end of man" and was aware of the transitoriness of the "pomps and vanities of this wicked world." He was not, however, the traditional dour Scot. Sir Andrew McPhail wrote of him:

> "If I were asked to state briefly the impression which remains with me most firmly, I should say it was one of continuous laughter. That is not true, of course, for in repose his face was heavy, his countenance more than ruddy; it was even of a "choleric" cast, and at times almost livid, especially when he was recovering from one of those attacks of asthma from which he habitually suffered. But his smile was his own, and it was ineffable. It filled the eyes, and illumined the face. It was the smile of sheer fun, of pure gaiety, of sincere playfulness, innocent of irony; with a tinge of sarcasm — never. When he allowed himself to speak of meanness in the profession, of dishonesty in men, of evil in the world, his face became formidable. The glow of his countenance deepened; his words were bitter, and the tones harsh. But the indignation would not last. The smile would come back. The effect was spoiled. Everyone laughed with him."[4]

McCrae was a companionable man who loved and enjoyed life, who used every minute of it, without thinking that enjoyment was an end in itself. But underneath the happy exterior was the continual sense of the ephemeral nature of happiness, perhaps developed by the tragic death of his first love. The struggle between human love and his sense of duty to the Divine troubled him until the end of his life. He chose the path of duty but in his poetry the spectre of death and its mockeries were always present. McCrae did not take his poetry seriously — it was a form of relaxation. For a man of his self-discipline no minute must be wasted, and so he wrote poems instead of limericks, and did fine sketches rather than doodles.

The poem *Anarchy*, which is different from his other verses, was written in response to the activities of the anarchists in the late 19th century. Anarchy welled up from the despair of the industrial working classes in their terrible conditions; anarchists had a vision of a stateless society, without government, private property, or corrupt institutions. They preached the necessity of violence to revolutionize a system they saw as completely evil, and felt that the oppressed classes needed awakening to the "Idea" by the "Propaganda of the Deed." Between 1894 and 1914 six heads of state were assassinated by anarchists. Most people saw anarchists as degenerates or lunatics. McCrae saw in them the sin of pride which occurred when men set themselves up as God.

Anarchy

I saw a city filled with lust and shame,
   Where men, like wolves, slunk through the grim half-light;
And sudden, in the midst of it, there came
   One who spoke boldly for the cause of Right.

And speaking fell before that brutish race
   Like some poor wren that shrieking eagles tear,
While brute Dishonour, with her bloodless face
   Stood by and smote his lips that moved in prayer.

"Speak not of God! In centuries that word
   Hath not been uttered! Our own king are we."
And God stretched forth his finger as He heard
   And o'er it cast a thousand leagues of sea.

Massey Magazine, 1897

William Osler and staff, Department of Medicine, Johns Hopkins Hospital 1903-1904. Osler's clinical associates and resident physicians are in the second row. From left to right: Campbell P. Howard, Thomas McCrae, William S. Thayer, William Osler, Thomas B. Futcher, Charles P. Emerson, and Rufus Cole. (From "The Chief, Doctor William Osler" by R. Palmer Howard. Canton, Mass.: Science History Publications, Watson Publishing International, 1983. With permission of R. Palmer Howard.)

CHAPTER FOUR
WILLIAM OSLER AND THE
JOHNS HOPKINS HOSPITAL: 1898-99

In 1898 McCrae graduated brilliantly with the gold medal from the University of Toronto medical school. He then worked briefly as resident house officer at the Toronto General Hospital, and in 1899 he went as an intern to the Johns Hopkins Hospital in Baltimore, following the example of a number of the foremost graduates of Toronto. John's brother Thomas had been working at Johns Hopkins as assistant resident since 1895 and had become a close associate of William Osler, but in 1899 Tom was studying at Gottingen in Germany.[1] John spent several months working in Baltimore, where he had been the previous summer, before going to McGill in the September of 1899 to study pathology as Governor's Fellow under Professor J.G. Adami.

William Osler was at the centre of the revolution in medicine and in medical teaching which occurred in the late 19th century in North America. He was a highly influential man with close links with the medical profession in Toronto and Montreal, and he had many of the attitudes and virtues which McCrae later displayed in his professional and personal life. It is highly likely that Osler had a strong influence on John McCrae, as he did on Tom McCrae and on his many other students.

Osler was an extraordinary man. He was born in Ontario in 1849, started his study of science and medicine in Toronto, and completed his medical degree at McGill. He graduated in 1872 from McGill, where he had had some good teachers at the old Montreal General Hospital; he described this hospital as a coccus- and rat-ridden building. In the 1870s while studying in London with Burdon-Sanderson, he made the major discovery of structures responsible for the clotting of blood platelets. Then he went on to study in Germany and Austria at a time when those countries represented the high-point in medical knowledge. He returned to McGill in 1874 "with the enlarged outlook that made him a vital factor in the great changes that were taking place in medicine."[2] Osler, like McCrae, was a reader of the Victorian "prophet" Thomas Carlyle; he was deeply affected by a sentence in *Sartor resartus*: "Our main business in life is not to see what lies dimly at a distance, but to do what lies clearly at hand." A man of great industry, Osler recommended keeping a notebook in which to jot down every point of interest. McCrae carried such notebooks and quickly filled them.

There are not sufficient superlatives to describe Osler's life and his effect on others; he was worshipped by his contemporaries with idolatrous zeal. Osler was influenced by the English 17th-century physician Thomas Brown and shared Brown's great humanism, if not his religion. Described as "God-like in his attributes" and praised for the "Christ-like quality in his nature," he was the best-known and loved physician of his generation in North America. A man of some humility, he emphasized that the poor must be cared for and that medical men must always be students.

He also believed that success in medicine depended on a thorough grounding in pathology; McCrae spent several years as a pathologist before turning to clinical medicine.

In 1889 Osler went to the Johns Hopkins Hospital in Baltimore, attracted as much by the method of organization there as by the hospital and the excellence of its staff. In contrast to the traditional structure of hospitals, Johns Hopkins was divided into units each of which was under the charge of a head or "Chief." The units were pathology, medicine, surgery, and gynecology.

Johns Hopkins, a Quaker businessman with railway interests, had left several million dollars to found a university and hospital. The teaching hospital opened in 1889. At that time there were five other medical schools in Baltimore, the best of which granted a diploma after two years of instruction. Professorships in these schools were given to the busiest general practitioners in the city. Osler attacked this system in open derision: "Is it to be wondered, considering this shocking laxity, that there is widespread distrust in the public of professional education, and that quacks, charlatans and imposters possess the land."[3] American medical education was fossilized, old-fashioned, and dangerous. Osler's ideal was "to build up a great clinic on Teutonic lines ... on the lines which have placed the scientific medicine of Germany in the forefront of the world."[4] Under Osler, the best of the French, English, and German ideas of medical teaching were incorporated at Johns Hopkins to make it rapidly the foremost medical school on the continent.

Osler knew the revolution which had occurred in medicine in his lifetime and to which he had contributed. After the funeral in 1912 of Lord Lister, the famous surgeon who introduced antiseptic surgery, he wrote: "Only those who have lived in the pre-Listerian days can appreciate the revolution which has taken place in surgery. In the seventies in the old Montreal General Hospital we passed through it."[5] Later he also wrote: "To have lived through a revolution, to have seen a new birth of science, a new dispensation for health, reorganized medical schools, remodelled hospitals, a new outlook for humanity, is not given to every generation."[6]

Against the exciting background of studying medicine at the leading medical school in North America there were other influences at work which were to affect John McCrae. In the 1890s, to the dismay of many, a wave of imperialism swept the United States. This was in part a result of the feeling that the United States had become a powerful nation. Many Americans shared the view of Senator Henry Cabot Lodge, who asserted proudly that "we are a great people; we control this continent; we are dominant in this hemisphere; we have too great an inheritance to be trifled with or parted with. It is ours to guard and extend."[7] President Cleveland's assertion of the Monroe Doctrine in 1895, following a dispute with Britain over Venezuela, led to a surge of jingoism in the United States and fears of an American invasion of Canada. Anti-British feeling abated when the American cruiser *Maine* blew up in Havana harbour and the United States declared war on Spain. An Anti-Imperialist League was formed in the United States but most Americans were attracted to jingoism, driven partly by a sense of the Almighty's plan to spread American ideals (and trade) to debased civilizations and decaying races. The sugar interests promoted this work and in 1898, at their instigation, Hawaii was annexed by the United States. The next year Rudyard Kipling's poem *The white man's burden* was published in *McClure's Magazine*. It was widely quoted to reconcile Americans to their imperial role. It was pasted in John McCrae's scrapbook.

In 1898 the Czar of Russia issued a call to all nations to join in an arms limitation conference. The Czar wrote that: "The intellectual and physical strength of nations, labour and capital alike, have been unproductively consumed in building terrible engines of destruction ... (which) will inevitably lead to the very cataclysm which it is designed to avert."[8] This proclamation was greeted warmly in the west, where it was seen as humanitarian and utopian. The swelling armaments industry in Europe was a cause of great concern; weapons were becoming deadlier each year and required matching by all armies. There was much pressure in England for disarmament.

A half-hearted international disarmament conference was held in The Hague in May 1899 at which an admiral of the British navy was heard to state that "the supremacy of the British Navy is the best security for the peace of the world."[9] MacCrae showed that he shared the admiral's feelings in a poem published in 1899 in the Toronto *Globe*. At the time this poem was published the outbreak of the second Boer War was gripping world attention.

Disarmament

One spake amid the nations, "Let us cease
    From darkening with strife the fair World's light,
We who are great in war be great in peace.
    No longer let us plead the cause by might."

But from a million British graves took birth
    A silent voice — the million spake as one —
"If ye have righted all the wrongs of earth
    Lay by the sword! Its work and ours is done."

Members of the Guelph Contingent to the South African War, January 1900. Lt. John McCrae standing at the front. (Public Archives of Canada, PA 28909)

CHAPTER FIVE
THE BOER WAR: 1899-1900

The Diamond Jubilee of Queen Victoria in 1897 marked the high-point of the British Empire, as the Boer War was to mark the beginning of its decline. By 1897 the British, by different means, "in a fit of absence of mind," had acquired dominion over one-quarter of the world. What had begun as an amateur brand of expansionism had become an official policy with widespread support in Britain. People talked of a Greater Britain and the term "New Imperialism" was coined. The jubilee unleashed a torrent of national arrogance — by the time of the Boer War Britain was the most envied and disliked of the great states. But Britain was lagging behind Germany and the United States in industrial production, and it was no longer the workshop of the world. Moreover, while Britannia still ruled the waves, other states were starting to build large navies. There was misgiving in Britain about the overconfident and pompous ideas of the New Imperialists, ideas summed up in Kipling's poem *Recessional*. It was a favourite poem of McCrae's.

In 1883 the Cambridge historian J.R. Sealey had published his influential book *The expansion of England*, which suggested that Europe was in a state of decline, and that within 50 years the United States and Czarist Russia "would completely dwarf such old European states as France and Germany, and depress them into second class."[1] He added that "they will do the same for England if at that time England still thinks of herself as a European state." It was his thinking which provided a philosophical basis for the New Imperialism and the Boer War.

In 1834 Britain had ordered the emancipation of all slaves in the Empire. In South Africa this action led to the Great Trek of 5,000 Boers across the Orange and Vaal Rivers, their goal being the formation of independent republics where political rights were denied to Africans. Britain had recognized the two Boer republics, the Transvaal and Orange Free State, but in 1877 it had annexed the Transvaal as the start of a process of federation in South Africa. The annexation was reversed in 1881, when the Boers heavily defeated a British army at Majuba. Later the discovery of gold in the Transvaal led to a flood of British gold-seekers. In 1895 some of the "gold-bugs," including Cecil Rhodes and Alfred Beit, financed from Rhodesia an attempted coup in the Transvaal. The Jameson raid ended in fiasco and public humiliation for Rhodes. Britons were shocked by the raid, but more by the telegram to the Boers from the Kaiser of Germany, who congratulated the Boers for repelling the invasion "without appealing to the help of friendly powers." The hostility of Germany shocked the British public, and the fleet was mobilized for a time.

In 1897 Sir Alfred Milner was sent out to South Africa as high commissioner by the secretary of state for the colonies, Joseph Chamberlain, "The Minister for Empire." Milner was a brilliant diplomat and a leader among the New Imperialists. He felt that British power was in decline, and he was determined to reassert it in the white part of the Empire, which he wanted to incorporate into a federated Greater Britain. Milner also wanted to unite the several South African colonies under the British Crown as a single self-governing white colony supported by well-treated black labour.

British public opinion was not in favour of a war to incorporate the Boer republics into the Empire; indeed, there was great resentment at the skullduggery of the gold-mine owners. The mandate given Milner by Chamberlain was to negotiate with the Boers so that British immigrants in the Transvaal, who outnumbered the Boers, could be granted political rights. Milner decided that war and not negotiation was the way to further his dream of a great white South Africa. He refused to compromise with the Boers in negotiations at Bloemfontein in June 1899, even though they granted him immense concessions. The gap between the two sides was minimal, but Milner's intransigence made a settlement impossible.

In England the issue for Chamberlain soon changed from one of gaining the franchise for Britons in the Boer colonies to one of British prestige. What was at stake was "the position of Great Britain in South Africa — and with it the estimate formed of our power and influence in the colonies and throughout the world."[2] War was declared by the Boers in October 1899. Ten thousand English troops were ordered to South Africa. By European standards the army was small, but it had an unequalled range of experience acquired in various "Butcher-and-Bolt" operations used in the acquisition of empire. Apart from the first Boer War, where they were defeated, and the Crimean War, the British had not fought Europeans since the Napoleonic era. Their remarkable successes in the field in the 70 years since had depended on regimental traditions, strong discipline, and the possession of superior firepower in battles with poorly armed natives. The British army was confident of its ability to defeat the Boers quickly. The declaration of war by the Boers was widely regarded in the Empire as preposterous and farcical.

The first months of the war saw a series of expensive British victories and disastrous British defeats. These culminated in Black Week in December 1899, when the Empire was stunned by British defeats at Colenso, Magersfontein, and Stormberg. Black Week provoked a burst of patriotism in the Empire and a wave of Anglophobia in Europe. In the autumn of 1899 Germany decided to double her fleet.

On 3 October 1899 the Canadian *Military Gazette* announced that Canada would supply troops for the war. This was denied by Prime Minister Wilfred Laurier, but before he had made his statement the Colonial Secretary had cabled from England to express his "high appreciation of the signal exhibition of the patriotic spirit of the people of Canada shown by offers to serve in South Africa."[3] No such offer had been made; however, despite opposition in Quebec, English Canadian demands for the dispatch of Canadian troops to

South Africa proved impossible to resist. On 18 October the government announced that it would equip and pay a volunteer force of 1,000 men, which sailed for South Africa at the end of that month. While greatly enjoying his work in Montreal, McCrae could not settle as he watched the progressive British defeats in South Africa. After the loss of Ladysmith he felt it his duty to go to the war. Encouraged by J G Adami and others, though opposed by Tom McCrae, he obtained permission to postpone his fellowship at McGill for a year. A letter to his mother describes his state when he thought that a second army contingent would not be formed:

> I see by to-night's bulletin that there is to be no second contingent. I feel sick with disappointment, and do not believe that I have ever been so disappointed in my life for ever since this business began I am certain there have not been fifteen minutes of my waking hours that it has not been in my mind. It has to come sooner or later. I shall not pray for peace in our time. One campaign might cure me, but nothing else ever will, unless it should be old age. I regret bitterly that I did not enlist with the first, for I doubt if ever another chance will offer like it. This is not said in ignorance of what the hardships would be.
>
> I am ashamed to say I am doing my work in a merely mechanical way. If they are taking surgeons on the other side, I have enough money to get myself across. If I knew any one over there who would do anything, I would certainly set about it. If I can get an appointment in England by going, I will go. My position here I do not count as an old boot in comparison.[4]

A second contingent, which included McCrae, was accepted in December during Black Week. Lord Strathcona paid for the equipment and costs of a further unit, the Canadian Mounted Rifles, made up mainly of North West Mounted Police.

The militia armoury in Guelph was made a recruiting point for the Royal Canadian Artillery (RCA) unit that was being sent to South Africa. Fifty-four men belonging to the 11th and 16th field batteries at Guelph joined as part of D Battery. Other batteries in the RCA unit were C and E. On 4 January the Guelph section was due to leave for Ottawa and a half-holiday was proclaimed in the city. In the morning and afternoon the men were drilled by McCrae who was their lieutenant. Afterwards photographs were taken and the men were given bibles. Senior officers gave speeches about obeying orders and acquitting themselves to the credit of Canada and the Empire, and McCrae was presented with a set of field glasses. All the local schoolboys marched with their teachers to the railway station for the departure. The city was widely decorated and many visitors came from the country areas. The contingent marched to the station through wild and cheering crowds. The marchers included artillery officers, the Wellington 30th Rifles, the Veterans of 1866, the City Council, the Highland Cadets, and the Fire Brigade. Fireworks were set off in the main square, and the jam of people was such that it was almost impossible to reach the station. Near the station a huge bonfire was lit on the ice on the river, and a band played *The British Grenadiers*, *The girl I left behind me*, and *God save the Queen*.

The Guelph section reached a bitterly cold Ottawa that day, where D Battery was formed. Lieutenant McCrae was put in charge of the right section, Lieutenant E.W.B. Morrison, who was to become a great friend of McCrae, was in charge of the left section, and a Captain Van Tuyl was in charge of the centre section. The battery consisted of 174 men, 29 riding horses, 108 draft horses, and six 12-pounder guns and ammunition. Each section had two guns. In Ottawa the battery camped on the Exhibition grounds, where the men painted their equipment khaki. Thirty thousand cheering people saw them off from Ottawa on 16 January, including Governor General Lord Minto and an unnamed but cheery American, who handed out cigars and flasks containing what was described in a Guelph newspaper as "a brown fluid."[4]

In Halifax, from where the unit was to sail, enthusiasm was again enormous. Ten thousand people a day visited the troops' camp. The contingent of 1,300 men left for South Africa on 20 January, after a crowd of 30,000 had cheered itself hoarse watching the embarkation parade.

D and E batteries were boarded on the *Laurentian*. The journey to Cape Town was marred by seasickness and by concern for the horses, which suffered in the poorly ventilated holds. Twenty-six horses died of pneumonia during the journey. Like most sea voyages, the journey became tedious, but it was enlivened by games, drilling, and gun firing. McCrae complained of the difficulty of commanding a volunteer militia force and was irritated by the government ban on alcohol. They landed in Africa on the 18th.

The English in Cape Town were jubilant because the siege of Kimberley had just been relieved and because in the previous three weeks 11,000 troops had landed. On 21 February the Canadian batteries and other colonial contingents, together with British regulars and volunteers, paraded through the town.

The RCA lines were visited by Rudyard Kipling, who was not recognized. On hearing this, the Chaplain, McCrae, and Morrison went to his hotel to see the man described by McCrae as the "high priest of it all."[5] They said that they were sorry to have missed him the day before. Kipling replied, "That's all right — I heard you cursing considerable — I could tell that you were up to your eyes in work."[6] After a few minutes talk he advised them to boil their water, and they shook hands. Kipling was one of the staunchest proponents of British imperialism. His verses and prose were read throughout the Empire; meeting Kipling was as exciting to McCrae as meeting the Queen.

McCrae enjoyed every minute of Cape Town — the physical work, the strange sights and smells, the excitement of mixing with the British regiments with those magical names which had thrilled him for so long — the "Buffs," "Seaforths," "Connaught," and "Black Watch." Cape Town was a menagerie of troops from all over the empire — Sikhs, Australians, Bombay Lancers, New Zealanders — all mingling with East Indians, Kaffirs, Coolies, Sudanese, Arabs, and Egyptians of the city. McCrae felt the power and size of the empire

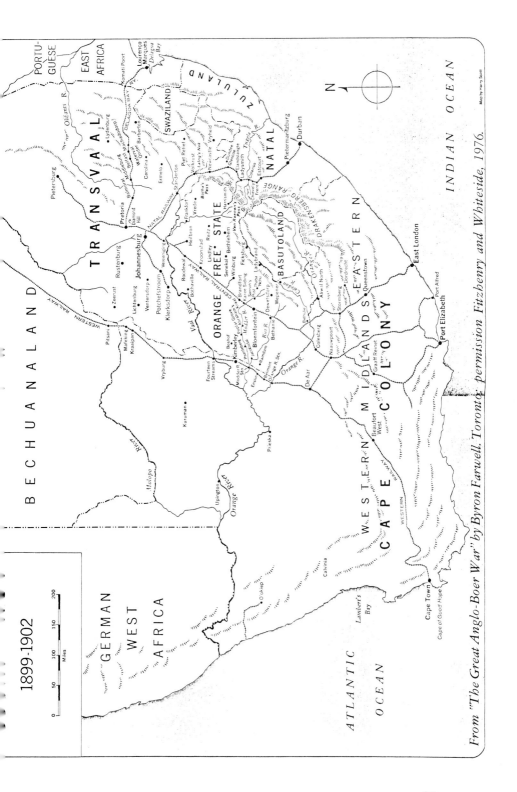

From "The Great Anglo-Boer War" by Byron Farwell. Toronto: permission Fitzhenry and Whiteside, 1976.

1899-1902

0 50 100 150 200
Miles

Map by Harry Scott

Lt. E.W.B. Morrison leading the Left Section, D Battery, Royal Canadian Artillery. Capetown, South Africa, 1900. (McCrae Birthplace Museum)

and he was thrilled by the sight of the "Sons of the Widow" under the "Brotherhood of the Union Jack."[6] He wrote home that he was "getting used to soldiering, and felt born to it."[7] All traces of his asthma had gone.

On the evening of 4 March the right and centre sections of D Battery left Cape Town, shortly after seeing the arrival of the Boer prisoners from the defeat at Paardeberg — "a dirty looking lot, smelt bad, all ages and all sizes, but mostly old men and young boys."[8] They arrived at Victoria West after journeying through the scrub country called the Karroo.

A rebellion had broken out in the northwest part of Cape Colony, around a town called Kenhardt. The British plan was that a group of about 1,000 men, including D Battery, would march from Victoria West to Kenhardt. There they would meet with a similar section from De Aar and together would overawe the rebels with their presence. The trip may have been a ruse to test the Canadians or to get them out of the way of the British army, which did not trust colonial troops. In McCrae's column there were D and E batteries, West Australians, New Zealanders, and Canadian Mounted Infantry. The rebels were reported to have 3,000 men and two guns. The column initially camped not in Victoria West, which was regarded as disloyal, but in a nearby sand plain that adjoined a Boer village. At night the men could see the Boers signalling from the low hills a few miles away, and shells were fused in readiness for action. Although they were on the edge of rebel country, the troops felt that the work was too tame — they wanted some real fighting.

On 14 March the column left the camp to make the hardest and longest march of the war. The Canadians were the backbone of the force, which consisted of 1,200 men, two machine guns, and twelve 12-pounder guns. The transport required to feed the column was a slow moving assortment of oxteams, mules, and donkeys stretching over three miles of desert and moving at three miles an hour. The trail was marked by bully beef tins and the bones of dead horses. Locusts obscured the sun and clouded the land like mist. To escape the heat the men marched by night, a ghostly procession made more eerie by the muffling of noise by the dust.

On 17 March the column reached Carnarvon, a little town in the Karoo. The 12 loyalists in the town gave them a great welcome; the 600 Boers were sullen but prepared tea and jam sandwiches. A compulsory church parade was held on Sunday, in the heat of the day, amid grumbling by the men. McCrae wrote, "The consolations of religion are all right, but a little common sense is not a bad thing in its way."[8]

Over the next days small columns left Carnarvon for Van Wyck's Vlei, travelling through Godforsaken country of dust and bad water. They marched from 4 a.m. to miday and again in the evening — 12 to 30 miles a day depending on the sand and their bullocks. The New Zealand column and McCrae entered Van Wyck's Vlei and captured three rebels. The columns reunited in this town for the march to Kenhardt. To add to the misery of that journey, it poured rain for days. McCrae was almost drowned when his horse fell on him in the water. He was praised for his work in these crossings. The trip to Kenhardt took 11 days, during which time the horses needed constant care. Rations fell to five pounds of wheat and five pounds of chaff per day, and the horses were too tired to eat. The gunners rested for ten minutes every hour, and dismounted and walked ten minutes every hour. Although eventually praised, McCrae was criticized at the time for being overcareful in his treatment of the horses.

Kenhardt was occupied by McCrae and 250 men of the Canadian Mounted Infantry. To their intense disappointment, they discovered a miserable village with a population of only 12 whites and the rest natives. They loyally paraded in the village, gave three cheers for the Queen and the British Empire, and ran up the flag. During their five-day stay in Kenhardt the men became ill with dysentry and rheumatism. In addition they were demoralized by the terrible country, the hardness of the march, and the miserable village they reached. There were cases of drunkenness so serious that the Canadian troops were threatened with being sent back to Canada.

On 5 April a telegram arrived from Lord Kitchener stating that the men were needed at Bloemfontein. The march out was as tough as the march in and took 12 days. Because of McCrae's care D Battery lost five horses while other units lost more. They arrived at Victoria West on 17 April eager to see some fighting.

The following days were tedious as the men recovered from their journey. They received three months back pay but complained that they were the poorest paid of the colonials. The left and centre sections were set out for De Aar, while McCrae's section remained at Victoria guarding the railway line. His great complaint was of boredom — a series of gun drills and guard duties, with the stench of dead horses and sheep manure fires on the wind. Days became weeks, and McCrae was frantic in his frustration. His letters home speak of watching the City of London Imperial Volunteers going past in first-class carriages, and he commented that because of their influence these men got to the fighting. He even wondered whether the battery was being punished for the drunkenness at Kenhardt. To relieve the tedium he kept a book in which he collected gems of profanity, being particularly fascinated by the language of one sergeant-major; in later years McCrae was known to use some of these phrases when angry or exasperated.

McCrae visited the hospital at De Aar, and was shocked. He wrote home, "No RAMC (Royal Army Medical Corps) or other MC for me; there is a big breach, and the medicals are on the far side of it."[9] Of the hospital he wrote: "For absolute neglect and rotten administration, it is a model. I am ashamed of some members of my profession.... Every day there are from 15-30 Tommies dying from fever and dysentry. Every one that dies is sewn up in a blanket, and 4 shillings are taken out of the pay for the blanket. The soldiers game is not what it is cracked up to be."

After Pretoria was captured it was assumed that the war would be over. However, there was still highly effective guerilla activity in the Orange Free State by the Boers under De Wet, and in the Transvaal by the Boers under Botha. To their delight, the whole of D Battery was ordered to Pretoria to assist in capturing De Wet. During the march to Sannah's Post the men passed terrible sights, which deeply affected McCrae, left from the ambush by De Wet of General Broadwood and 1,700 British troops, a fight in which seven guns were captured and 428 prisoners taken by the Boers. In mid July they reached Pretoria and joined the force of General Ian Hamilton.

On 17 July D Battery was attached to General Cunningham's brigade, and it started to see some fighting against De Wet's 800 guerillas. Cunningham's column consisted of 4,500 infantry with the six guns of D Battery, two pompom guns, and some larger guns. The transport line of mules, horses, and oxen was six miles long. They were fired on a few times but failed to make contact with the Boers, though they could see their heliographic signalling in the distance. On the fourth day of the advance they were fired on a few times by Boer artillery. Morrison returned the fire. After advancing a further four miles they were fired on again; McCrae and Morrison responded with 40 to 50 rounds from their four guns. The Boers returned 20 to 25 shells, some of them

Officers of the "Kenhardt Column" South Africa, 1900. John McCrae is second from left in the middle row. (Public Archives of Canada, C 19918)

coming close and hitting one wagon. The British and colonials later found four dead Boer soldiers and nine freshly dug graves where the enemy had been. The next day, Sunday, they marched forward on a four-mile front and made desultory contact with the Boers. They had marched 80 miles in one week. On Monday the column was halted by heliograph orders from Field Marshall Lord Roberts. Shortly afterwards McCrae was ordered to take the right section up a slope 1½ miles away, where he was shown a target of 70 Boers on a ridge at 4,000 yards distance. The section arrived after galloping over stony ground and the shooting began. McCrae's men fired four percussion shells, found the range, and then fired 12 shrapnel shells, killing one man. After firing six unpleasantly close shrapnel shells, the Boers retreated as was their practice. D Battery were later officially complimented on their performance; it was said that the men acquitted themselves "as well as any Imperial Battery."[10] Despite the danger, McCrae was exhilarated by his first taste of fighting.

The following days the hard march continued through the ruined countryside. Most of the farms in the district were deserted; no crops or farm animals were seen. Goods were available at exorbitant prices, and the Boer households, consisting of old men, women, and children, were in misery. The column eventually reached Balmoral railway station but without its transport and the men went to bed without food and blankets. The night was exceptionally cold; 10 men and 200 of the exhausted horses and mules died of exposure. The transport arrived the following day, and the men had their first sight of the legendary Lord Roberts and his famous chief of staff, Lord Kitchener of Khartoum.

Sketch of guns on Fusillier Hill, Penaarsport, August 1900, by John McCrae. (McCrae Birthplace Museum)

The next few days they spent at Penaarspoort, where McCrae and Morrison took turns manning two guns perched on a kopje guarding the camp below. Boers were occasionally sighted but well out of range for the guns. The Canadians spent their time searching the country with field glasses, reading Tennyson's poems, and eating. Some of the tinned food brought from Canada was bad and McCrae developed food poisoning. After two weeks on top of Fusilier Hill, they became bored again. They were short of rations for themselves and their animals, but they could hear fighting a few miles away and were desperate to join it. Under these circumstances, keeping his 45 men happy must have tried McCrae.

After three weeks they were ordered to the front. They brought down the guns with difficulty in the night and marched with some Imperial Yeomanry ("rotten, and cursed by the Army") to Erstafabriken, where McCrae reported to Colonel Otter, leader of the First Canadian Contingent, and then put the guns and horses on the train for Belfast, picking up Morrison's section in Pretoria on the way. They reached Belfast station at 3 p.m. and immediately came under Boer fire. McCrae's section went immediately from the train to a line of trenches 200 yards from the station, and into action. The enemy was pushed back by General Buller's forces, but covered their retreat with a Long Tom gun firing from a railway track, one 6-inch shell actually falling 10 yards behind McCrae's guns. The Boers suffered heavily from the British guns which were firing shells loaded with lyddite explosive. This defeat of the Boer General Botha and his 7,000 men was a crushing victory for Lord Roberts; the British army was learning some of the tactics needed for success. Still, McCrae and Morrison were critical of the British style of fighting — of using too many frontal attacks and of advancing in line without using cover. Canadians performed better and lost fewer men.

After the firing ceased, Lord Roberts himself appeared and formally inspected the Battery. He said to the right section, "I promised to get you up, and I have done so" referring to complaints that the Canadians were seeing no real fighting. The Battery, together with the men of the Gordon Highlanders and the Royal Scots Greys, held its first Presbyterian service since leaving Canada. Some of the officers described McCrae's group as "McCrae and his Covenanters," a fact to which he referred with pleasure. He enjoyed mixing with and feeling an equal of officers of the famous British regiments.

A week after the battle of Belfast the right section advanced with a battalion of Gordon Highlanders to take part in the battle of Lydenburg. The slow advance through large hills was resisted by Boer snipers. On 6 September McCrae and his men were in the advance acting as horse artillery with the 2nd Cavalry Brigade. They came into action several times during the day, firing at the retreating enemy. Near Lydenberg they were fired on by a Boer gun, and they retreated unwillingly, under generals' orders, for three miles. The horses were exhausted, having pulled the guns for 25 miles, mostly on the trot.

The assault on the Boer positions at Lydenberg relied on the classic British tactics of a frontal attack and an outflanking approach. On 7 September the 18th Hussars with D Battery entered the small town of Lydenburg, while Hamilton's main force went west of the town. D Battery was shelled from Boer positions by five guns on ridges to the east of the town, and as the force retired it was pursued by shells. The men classed the Boers as good gunners, though some of their shells failed to explode.

The next day McCrae's men again advanced with cavalry through the town of Lydenburg, and they came into action when they were fired on by a group of mounted Boers. After dispersing these Boers, they returned to camp where they were fired on, from 2 p.m. until dark, by guns on the hills. Some men of the Irish Regiment were killed and the transport was moved out. McCrae wrote that "the Kaffir driver is quick when the fear of death lies before him — not otherwise."[10] The shelling from five guns 10,000 yards away was accurate, and one shell arrived every two or three minutes. McCrae's section could see the flash and smoke of the gun firing at them. Shrapnel often burst over them. McCrae said of this time: "The waiting under fire is very hard — a constant strain — though nobody lets on it is so worrying. The suspense of waiting for shell after shell to burst over your head is very hard work. There were many narrow escapes, and we have been fortunate...."[11] And then in typical fashion he went on to write of the animals. "Our dogs are very sociable. Dolly, Grit, Tory, — and Kitty the monkey rides the off-horse on the fore-wagon."

A general attack was ordered on the hill from which the enemy had fired at them the day before. The cavalry of Buller and Hamilton attacked in three columns and the infantry advanced in five or six lines of men. The attack was resisted by the Boers. McCrae had a perfect view of the fighting and his section came into action during the day. Firing stopped at 4 p.m., when the bulk of the enemy followed their usual practice of melting away; the battle of Lydenburg was over. McCrae's section retired down the hill to camp — they had not had their clothes off for 10 days.

After a short time the advance continued, hampered by the snipers and the veldt fires set by the Boers, but the horses of McCrae's section were in such poor condition that the unit was detached for a few days. The enormous wastage of horses and oxen through disease, starvation, and exhaustion was one of the daily features of the war which appalled McCrae. The average life of a British horse in South Africa was six weeks.

McCrae's men rested for a few days at Godwan Station, where they were given a two-ton ammunition wagon, two donkeys, and three broken-down mules to replace their losses. After getting rid of the wagon they marched as escort of a regiment through difficult country to Nelspruit. There the section's guns and horses were put on the train for the base camp of Machadodorp. They took part in some small skirmishes around the camp over the next days. On 8 October the right section went on reconnaissance to Elands Kop and sighted some Boers. The men went into action on the gallop, firing at the Boers as they scattered. The range was long and there was a gusty wind, but some shells were well planted despite the difficult ground. Their work was greatly praised.

The next month was spent guarding the railroad in or near Machadodorp, a task made difficult by heavy thunderstorms with hailstones which drove the horses crazy. Dead oxen near the camp attracted flies, which got in the jam. With no news, no orders, and no mail, the section again became intensely bored. Several men developed fever and dystentry ; the first Guelph man died, of enteric fever. The men talked of going home. McCrae was asked to stay for a further six months but declined. While the right section was waiting, Lieutenant Morrison's section was burning farms in the Transvaal and Morrison became involved in a fight to save his guns, an affair for which he was awarded the Distinguished Service Order for gallantry.

The general opinion in the British army was that the war was virtually over. The Canadians did not agree since they respected the Boers as good and clever fighters; however, their wish to return home was soon granted. They left South Africa and reached Halifax in early January 1901.

McCrae came in for special praise for his conduct during the war. His commanding officer said of him: "An exceptionally clever officer and a perfect gentleman. I cannot speak too highly of the service rendered by Lieutenants McCrae and Morrison."[12] The men described McCrae as the "constant companion and friend of the men. The life of the camp, sang songs and kept the boys cheerful when there was little to feel cheerful about. The boys think he is alright.... The most popular officer of the lot."[13]

The train carrying McCrae's section was cheered at the stations on its route to Guelph. On 11 January McCrae briefly met his McGill friends in Montreal before the train moved on to Toronto. He met his parents at a station just outside Guelph. The enthusiasm of the crowds at the station was described as whiteheat; the station was lit by arc-lights, the crowd roared as the train pulled in, and the band struck up. A procession through the town was led by McCrae in a cab with the mayor, though at times he was shouldered through the streets. Fireworks were let off, and the parade, led by a piper, included the Wellington Rifles, the Field Artillery, Highland Cadets, the City Council, school board officials, and others. At city hall they were welcomed by the mayor, who said that "the blood of our Canadian sons spilt upon the veldt of South Africa has been the means of cementing in inseparable bonds the Greater Britain.... Our beloved Queen has no more loyal defenders and British supremacy no more loyal supporters than the men of the Right section of D Battery."[14]

In a dinner given two months earlier for an invalided member of D section, Colonel David McCrae had said that the Guelph contingent were "fighting for the honour and unity of Empire in South Africa and, if not quite, they had nearly made Canada a nation. The whole empire, nay, the whole world were watching to see what manner of men we were, to see if the lion's whelps were of the same stuff as the old lion himself. The idea of the closer union of the Empire was fastening itself on the minds of the legislators."[15]

McCrae later wrote briefly about the Boer war without the imperialist rhetoric of his father, although he would not have disagreed with him about the significance of the conflict. He emphasized the price paid for the acquisition of empire, and he knew the cost of war.

> The red patch on the map of South Africa has grown, the addition having been purchased at a price.... Empire consists not only in Courts and Parliaments, in diplomatic oaths of alliance, but in poor cattle that drag their heavy wagons in pathetic silence until they die in the yoke, and gallant horses that bear the labour and heat of the day, in a struggle that was not of their making, for glory cannot appeal to them, until they, too, get honourably discharged from the service of the King.... In the field there are a thousand things that speak of the cost of war, the cost in

treasure; but there is an echo, even at home, in the rows of boyish faces, that appear week after week, in the illustrated magazines, with the inscription 'killed at —', or 'dead of wounds' — in sickening regularity, that speak of gaps in the stately homes of England, and, by inference, — of the other gaps, tenfold, in her cottages.

The same evening I attended service in the Cathedral ... there was a strange appropriateness that one of the hymns should be

'Conquering Kings their titles take
From the foes they captive make.'

for, stretching over the hill from the south wall in long dark rows, lay two thousand graves, where men slept that King Death had led captive, who were done with Kingdoms and republics; men whose message goes to the Empire, to the voice of a new colony that they had won by blood, — 'O stranger, go thou; and tell our people that we are lying here having obeyed their words.'[16]

The Boer War dragged on for another 1½ years, and was marked by the establishment of "concentration camps" by the British to contain captured Boers and their families. The cost was 100,000 casualties among 365,693 imperial and 82,742 colonial soldiers, and 400,000 horses, mules, and donkeys. More than 22,000 men died, 5,744 in action and 16,168 from wounds or disease. There were 7,000 deaths of fighting men among the total Boer population of 87,365; an estimated 18,000-28,000 Boer men, women, and children died in the concentration camps. The number of blacks slughtered by the Boers was uncounted.

McCrae never talked of his Boer War days. He had done his duty well and had been an excellent officer. He came back from the conflict fit and matured. It has been said of him that he hated war; certainly he saw his share of war's tragedies and waste in South Africa. He had learned that most wars consist of 90% boredom and 10% action, that the British army needed reorganization, and that the Canadian army was the equal of the British. The sights associated with the Boer War — the burned farms, the wrecked trains, the dead horses and oxen, and the graves filled with soldiers dead of enteric fever — would remain in his memory together with the exhilaration of working guns under fire. Most of the second contingent had had no desire to continue the fight after its term of duty was over. The Canadians had no taste for imprisoning women and children or for the scorched earth policy. McCrae was a man who felt that evil must be fought wherever it occurred and was prepared to lay down his life in the fight, but he remained ambivalent in his attitude to his adventures in the Boer War.

In 1901 McCrae was promoted to captain in the 16th Battery, 1st Brigade of Artillery, and in 1902 to major of the battery. He resigned in 1904, doing no more soldiering until 1914.

CHAPTER SIX
THE EARLY YEARS IN MONTREAL: 1901-05

In early 1901 McCrae returned to Montreal to study pathology with J.G. Adami, professor of pathology at McGill University and pathologist at the Royal Victoria Hospital. He spent the next four years studying pathology and establishing a reputation for excellence. It was a time when the medical school at McGill, with the associated Montreal General Hospital, was a major medical centre in North America.

The pathology and public health laboratories of McGill's medical faculty were built and equipped by J.H.R. Molson in 1893 in response to the endowment of chairs in these subjects by Sir Donald Smith, later Lord Strathcona. The men and women associated with the practice and teaching of pathology when McCrae arrived were gifted people with whom he became firm friends.

John George Adami was a man of charm and culture, a leader in the fields of pathology and medical education. He was born in England in 1862 and studied at Cambridge in the days of the renaissance stimulated by Darwin and Huxley, and he was nurtured by his teacher and friend, the physiologist Michael Foster. In 1889, while investigating an outbreak of rabies in a local deer herd, Adami sliced his hand cutting through a deer's brain. He left immediately for the Pasteur Institute in Paris for a life-saving series of injections, a miracle cure at the time. The following year he worked as a student in Paris with Roux, Metchnikoff, and Pasteur. He so appreciated this opportunity that, when he went to McGill in 1892, he established two fellowships with rules identical to those under which he had studied in Paris. McCrae, Oskar Klotz, and a succession of other young pathologists worked with him while holding these fellowships.

In 1892 this study of pathology was in its rudimentary stage in Montreal. There had been little organized effort to recognize the prime place of pathology and bacteriology in medicine. Adami arrived in Canada "just as laboratories of pathology and bacteriology were becoming seriously regarded as essential to the training of medical students."[1] Adami was pathologist in the new pathology laboratories at the Royal Victoria Hospital and taught pathology at McGill.

Adami's ambition was to found a school of pathology at McGill. He emphasized medical principles, history, and research, as well as the critical link between pathology and clinical medicine. His lectures were described as witty and original. From his own pocket he furnished a library in the Molson Laboratories of Pathology and Bacteriology. He encouraged his students "to view each problem as one demanding solution in his own hands."[2] He revitalized the Pathology Museum, which still contained some of Osler's preserved specimens, and took an active part in the life of the university. He helped found the University Club and the Lister Club, contributed to the Montreal Medico-Chirugical Society, and helped to run the *Montreal Medical Journal*. A new scientific spirit was evident in the medical school from the time of his arrival; it was said that "what Osler had done some 15-20 years previously in advancing knowledge and stimulating research was ... revived under Adami in later years."[3] Adami was also a cultured man, with a genius for making friends. "Few men in Montreal at the time had a wider knowledge of general literature or a better taste in art. His home was always a meeting ground for cultured people ... (he showed) a genuine taste for things that were good."[4] He was a man after McCrae's own heart.

The pathologist at the Montreal General Hospital was Wyatt Johnston, who while a medical student had been Osler's laboratory assistant, helping him in his autopsies in private houses in the slums of Montreal. Like many others, Johnston was inspired by Osler with an enthusiasm and a love of science, and an ambition to master pathology. He graduated from McGill in 1884 and studied in Berlin with Virchow in 1885 before returning to Montreal as demonstrator in pathology and lecturer in bacteriology.

Also associated with the pathology department at McGill was Dr Maude Abbott, a few years older than McCrae. She was in the first women's class admitted to McGill, in the Faculty of Arts, but as a woman had been unable to study medicine at McGill. Instead she studied medicine at Bishop's College and graduated in 1894. After doing postgraduate work in Germany, Austria, and Switzerland, she returned in 1897 to Montreal, where she began to practise medicine although she was determined to join the Medical Faculty at McGill. Dr Abbott worked at the Royal Victoria Hospital with Adami and Dr C.F. Martin, and in 1898 she was appointed assistant curator of the Medical Museum. Encouragement by Osler in late 1898 stimulated her to devote herself to the museum, of which she was appointed curator in 1901.

As Governor's Fellow in pathology and resident assistant pathologist, McCrae had the dual function of research work in the Medical Faculty laboratories at McGill and autopsy duties at the Montreal General Hospital. He carried out postmortem examinations of many cases of typhoid and tuberculosis, and of a lesser number of cases of peritonitis, poisoning, burns, and accidents. The autopsy book of the Montreal General Hospital volume for 1901 has the following inscription, written in early 1902 by McCrae:

> Here begynneth ye Booke of ye Deade, wherin is fayrely set foorth ye last state of four Hundred and seventeen persones, that have departed from this lyfe; wherein be tabled diverse and straunge and fearsome condicions that have ledde to ye same final ende: God have them of his grace.

> Our lyfe is but a Winter's Day.
> Some only breadfast and away.
> Others to dinner stay, and are fulle fedde.

The oldest man but suppes, and goes to bedde.
Large is his dette, that lingers out the day.
He that goes soonest has the least to pay!!

The source of the verse is not known, but it is of ancient origin. The last line may or may not be McCrae's since it differs from other published versions of the poem.[5]

McCrae's ability as a research scientist was summed up in typical fashion by his friend Andrew MacPhail:

In spite, or rather by reason, of his various attainments John McCrae never developed or rather degenerated into the type of pure scientist.... For the laboratory he had neither the mind nor the hands.... He wrote much, and often, upon medical problems. The papers ... testify to his industry rather than his invention and discovery, but they have made his name known in every textbook of medicine.[6]

In 1902 Wyatt Johnston died suddenly, and McCrae was appointed in his place as resident pathologist at the Montreal General Hospital. He was later appointed as assistant pathologist to the Royal Victoria Hospital.

The Royal Victoria Hospital had been founded in 1887 by the cousins Sir George Stephens and Sir Donald Smith in honour of the Queen's Golden Jubilee. Both men had made a fortune from railways, and they each donated half a million dollars to the hospital. Resident interns at the Royal Victoria when McCrae was appointed included his friend E.W. Archibald and C.B. Keenan, recently returned with a DSO from his medical duties with Strathcona's Horse in South Africa.

The Governor's Fellow in pathology who replaced McCrae at McGill was Oskar Klotz, a recent graduate of the University of Toronto, who became a firm friend. He followed McCrae as assistant pathologist at the Royal Victoria in 1905 when McCrae left to practise medicine. Klotz described some of their work in teaching pathology to medical students; McCrae or Klotz used to do autopsies, and Adami made the commentary, trying to relate clinical findings to the pathological process.

Jack McCrae was very helpful in these discussions, as he possessed a direct and logical mind, and a snappy comment which savoured of Carlyleism. McCrae's interests were partly clinical and in training pathological; he could visualize the clinical events and then from our findings he would bring some coordination of the several views. Adami was very appreciative of the value of McCrae's association, and our discussion, beginning with a topic at the autopsy table, was often prolonged long past the hour for dinner. Then often Adami would join us....

At the beginning of the century there was an unusual group of young men growing up in the various branches of Medicine. Almost every department was represented by keen young men, all of whom had served

Dr. Oskar Klotz. Taken 1920-1930. (Public Archives of Canada, PA 123480)

an extended post-graduate training both at home and abroad. These men occupying junior positions at the Royal Victoria Hospital or at the Montreal General Hospital became banded together in a social organisation named the Krausmanian Club — the name originated after a dull evening of quasi-scientific discussion on tuberculosis. McCrae, Klotz, Turner, Little, White, McKee, Campbell Howard, Francis, Archibald and others betook themselves to Krausman's restaurant, where matters practical, philosophical and social were discussed over the cups into the small hours of the night. This group met regularly once a month for a number of years, and Adami ... (was) one of the few of the senior members of the McGill Faculty who were admitted.[7]

McCrae was responsible for teaching both bacteriology and pathology to medical students. H.O. Howitt, his friend from Guelph, described how:

On Saturdays he demonstrated pathological specimens to students. Jack McCrae's ability to make lucid these findings and to explain the reasons in a logical and brief way, so that the students could easily digest and remember after a lecture what had been said, made these demonstrations very popular with the students. No student ever missed them. It was the reputation which he created at those Saturday demonstrations that largely influenced his future.

In my third year he demonstrated in Histology and Bacteriology. I am forever grateful for the assistance Jack McCrae gave me in making easy a subject which at first was very difficult for me. To be able to do so was his great gift and one of the reasons for his popularity with the students. I remember one day in the bacteriological laboratory we were working with tetanus, the germ that causes lockjaw. I had a tube in my hand containing a culture of tetanus, which I thought Jack McCrae told me to drop. I promptly did so, the tube crashed, and broke on the floor. There was not a smile on his face, but a look of sternness, and severity. He made a remark which even today would have to be printed with words omitted, and asterisks substituted. I protested that I had done what he told me to do. For a moment we stood facing each other; suddenly his expression changed, and the smile reappeared, and with his eyes fixed on mine he said: 'The first duty of a soldier is to obey, you did it.'[8]

McCrae's hot temper could flash when he felt patients were jeopardized through carelessness, or when professional standards were lacking.

As a teacher McCrae was outstanding, if dogmatic. Oskar Klotz wrote:

John McCrae was a born teacher. He loved the simple exposition of the pathology of disease and avoided at all times beclouding the subject with the abstruse and intricate. His demonstrations were impressive and sharp was his criticism, each point being made with a snap which reminded one that he was a student of Carlyle. If contrast was required in teaching it was used even to the grotesque.... I have repeatedly met students who sat under him and they never stinted their praise of his teaching.... The ward teaching was his particular delight, and when didactic lectures fell to his lot he converted them as nearly as possible into practical demonstrations by bringing as much pathological material to the lecture room as possible. The students loved him for the interest he always displayed in their difficulties and because he showed the human side of medicine. They learned from him the unselfish duty of the physician to human distress in all walks of life. They loved him, too, because he never feared to step from the dignity of the teacher to the level of the student.[9]

Between 1903 and 1912 a group of the McGill medical teaching staff served as special professors at the University of Vermont Medical College. They went to Burlington, Vermont, on the morning train and returned in the evening. McCrae lectured there in pathology from 1903-1911. He was regarded as the chief of the lecturers since he had an encyclopaedic knowledge and he filled in for others when they could not go. In his early articles he took pride in calling himself a professor of pathology at the University of Vermont.

He published one poem in 1903. It was entitled *Upon Watts' picture, "Sic transit"*.

> *"What I spent I had; what I saved, I lost; what I gave, I have."*

But yesterday the tourney, all the eager joy of life,
  The waving of the banners, and the rattle of the spears,
The clash of sword and harness, and the madness of the strife;
  To-night begin the silence and the peace of endless years.

(One sings within.)

But yesterday the glory and the prize,
  And best of all, to lay it at her feet,
To find my guerdon in her speaking eyes:
  I grudge them not, — they pass, albeit sweet.

The ring of spears, the winning of the fight,
  The careless song, the cup, the love of friends,
The earth in spring — to live, to feel the light —
  'Twas good the while it lasted: here it ends.

Remain the well-wrought deed in honour done,
  The dole for Christ's dear sake, the words that fall
In kindliness upon some outcast one, —
  They seemed so little: now they are my All.

University Magazine, 1903

By 1904 the medical staff at the Royal Victoria Hospital had reached a substantial size and it was decided to create a rank between the assistant physician or surgeon, and the more junior clinical assistant within each specialty. McCrae and two other colleagues were appointed associates in medicine. There was bitterness in the Montreal General Hospital, where it was felt that their better men were being poached by the Royal Victoria. In 1904 McCrae studied in England for some months, possibly to make a change from pathology to clinical medicine easier, and by examination became a licentiate of the Royal College of Physicians. He was succeeded as assistant pathologist at the Royal Victoria Hospital by Klotz, though McCrae seems for a time to have held both this appointment and his new one as associate in medicine. in 1905 he was appointed pathologist to the Montreal Foundling and Baby Hospital.

In late 1904 McCrae was asked to give the address at the opening of the new session of the Medical Faculty of the University of Vermont, an honour for one of his age. The address was published the next year in the *Montreal Medical Journal*, with the title "The Privileges of Medicine." It is a summary of McCrae's ideals and faith and includes the paragraph:

> Someone has well remarked that your poor patients have one claim upon you that your rich ones have not — their poverty.... I have refrained from putting this on a religious basis, though it is perhaps the very essence of religion; but it has often seemed to me that, when at the Judgement Day those surprised faces look up and say, 'Lord, when saw we Thee hungered and fed Thee? or thirsty and gave Thee drink? a stranger and took Thee in, or naked and clothed Thee?' and there meets them that Warrant-Royal of all Charity, 'Inasmuch as ye did it unto the least of these,' among those faces will be many a general practitioner, many a man unknown to the scroll of fame, but whose name, nevertheless, hangs on the wall of our Lodge! Is membership in this lodge no privilege?[10]

In 1905 McCrae published the poem *The pilgrims*, in which he returned to his gloomy theme of death as the reward for a life of Christian struggle. McCrae's public character was not as dour as his poetry suggests; he was described by his friends and acquaintances as charming, jovial, kindly, and sparkling. These qualities, however, were superimposed on what was a serious view of the world, perhaps even cultivated out of a sense of religious duty.

The pilgrims

An uphill path, sun-gleams between the showers,
    Where every beam that broke the leaden sky
Lit other hills with fairer ways than ours;
    Some clustered graves where half our memories lie;
        And this was Life.

Wherein we did another's burden seek,
    The tired feet we helped upon the road,
The hand we gave the weary and the weak,
    The miles we lightened one another's load,
When, faint to falling, onward yet we strode:
            This too was Life.

Till, at the upland, as we turned to go
    Amid fair meadows, dusky in the night,
The mists fell back upon the road below;
    Broke on our tired eyes the western light;
The very graves were for a moment bright:
            And this was Death.

University Magazine, 1905

A final poem of this period, also concerned with death but more optimistic than *The pilgrims*, was *The dying of Père Pierre*.

The dying of Père Pierre

...with two other priests; the same night he died,
and was buried by the shores of the lake that bears his name.
            Chronicle

Nay, grieve not that ye can no honour give
    To these poor bones that presently must be
But carrion; since I have sought to live
    Upon God's earth, as He hath guided me,
I shall not lack! Where would ye have me lie?
    High heaven is higher than cathedral nave:
Do men paint chancels fairer than the sky?
    Beside the darkened lake they made his grave,
Below the altar of the hills; and night
    Swung incense clouds of mist in creeping lines
That twisted through the tree-trunks, where the light
    Groped through the arches of the silent pines:
And he, beside the lonely path he trod,
Lay, tombed in splendour, in the House of God.

University Magazine, 1904

CHAPTER SEVEN
CHRONICLES OF WORK: 1906-10

The years 1906 to 1910 were full as McCrae carried out his duties as a physician and teacher. From 1905 his medical practice was mostly clinical. McCrae had a remarkable capacity for work but somehow managed to remain a companion and friend. His ability to make use of the odd half-hour was described as phenomenal.

Sir Andrew Macphail wrote of these years:

> Taken together his letters and diaries are a revelation of the heroic struggle by which a man gains a footing in a strange place in that most particular of all professions ... the method is simple. It is all disclosed in his words, 'I have never refused any work that was given me to do.' These records are mainly a chronicle of work. Outdoor clinics, laboratory tasks, post-mortems, demonstrating, teaching, lecturing, attendance upon the sick in wards and homes, meetings, conventions, papers, addresses, editing, reviewing — the very remembrance of such a career is enough to appal the stoutest heart.
>
> But John McCrae was never appalled. He went about his work gaily, never busy, never idle. Every minute was pressed into service, and every hour was made to count.[1]

McCrae's friend Stephen Leacock wrote:

> No man of our circle worked harder than did John McCrae. Yet he seemed to find time for everything, and contrived somehow to fill in the spare moments of a busy life with the reveries of a poet....
>
> He was in great demand at Montreal dinner parties ... fund of stories ... never exhausted ... the treasure of his hostess — a man of the greatest in eating and drinking, his amusements abhorred late hours and he kept himself, mind and body, in the training of an athlete.[2]

Macphail also described McCrae's popularity:

> Wherever he lived he was a social figure. When he sat at table the dinner was never dull. The entertainment he offered was not missed by the dullest intelligence. His contribution was merely 'stories,' and these stories in endless succession were told in a spirit of frank fun. They were not illustrative, admonitory, or horatory. They were just amusing, and always fresh. This gift he acquired from his mother, who had that rare charm of mimicry without mockery, and caricature without malice.[3]

McCrae was renowned as a story teller: "the repertoire (was) endless and the variety infinite, suitable in the parlour or the hunting trip as the occasion demanded."

Clinic at the Royal Alexandra Hospital, Montreal. McCrae, on right, with students and patients. (McCrae Birthplace Museum)

In 1908 McCrae was appointed physician to the Royal Alexandra Hospital for Infectious Diseases. He became interested in documenting the cases of scarlet fever sent there, and wrote articles on these cases for the *Montreal Medical Journal* and the *Maritime Medical News*. He presented a talk on the subject at the conference of the Maritime Medical Association in the summer of 1908, describing the diseases of children at the Royal Alexandra; the death rate was 7%. "I think my earliest recollection is of a girl," McCrae said, "a relative of my own, falling over in a convulsion after a trifling attack of scarlet fever; the days in which her life hung in the balance are yet vividly in my mind."[4]

He wrote carefully and humorously on the disease:

Favouring the belief in a personal devil, one child of 3½ came in with diphtheria, caught scarlet fever, had chicken pox, got oedema of the glottis, was intubated a number of times, coughed up the tube one night, it rolled under the bed and could not be found; it was supposed she had swallowed it, tracheotomy saved her life; she developed bilateral otitis

52

and mastoiditis, had her mastoids trephined, and finally departed on the 116th day cured, but disconsolately wailing. The hospital staff bore the separation well.[5]

In 1909 McCrae was appointed lecturer in medicine at McGill, but he remained also lecturer in pathology. In that year he wrote several chapters for *Modern Medicine*, a ten-volume text edited by William Osler and Thomas McCrae. He also published a long article in the *Montreal Medical Journal* on "The Pirates of Medicine," a long historical description of quacks in medicine and in part an attack on modern quackery, particularly as it related to the sale of patent medicines. It is well written, and while he mentions "sober Thomas Carlyle" it has lost the Carlylean rhetoric of his earlier prose.

Of an early 19th-century London quack who unfortunately killed a young woman he wrote:

Sir Francis Brodie had asked Long if his lotion could give the Marquis of Anglesey a new leg in place of the one that that gallant soldier had lost at Waterloo. Long thought he could; the liniment was applied and succeeded in producing a big toe.... Long was sentenced to 250 pounds fine .. so he lived to fight another day and killed an old lady a few months later. In the case of the righteous man, his works follow him, but Long followed his works at the age of thirty-seven, of consumption, which he declined to have treated by his own methods. A costly monument holds him down in Kensal Green cemetary.

Of Count Cagliostro

At any rate, the King excused the Count from further residence in Paris, and the Count excused himself from paying his rent. He offered to light the town of London by sea water, which he could render inflammable as oil, but that cock would not fight, and in 1787 he left London for the last time, on this occasion forgetting his wife, who immediately made public his entire career.

McCrae summarised his article in typical fashion:

I have spoken of a few of the pirates of medicine, and though the ships are at time prosperous, the keels that carry the regular flag win ultimately. We are not all line-of-battle ships, but a little one gun sloop with the ensign is more honourable than a 40-gun frigate that is a buccaneer.[6]

In 1909 McCrae's good friend Oskar Klotz left the Royal Victoria Hospital to become professor of pathology and bacteriology at the University of Pittsburgh. McCrae's letters were kept by Klotz and give an idea of his life at that time. They bring alive some of the vigour of the man in a way that the almost idolatrous regard by his contemporaries after his death does not. The blanks left in the letters are McCrae's.

A --- of a lot of work to do, but might be worse. I got the bloody Lister (medical society started by Adami) in for Monday last ... Taking whole class 4-6 on Tuesday and Thursday and that's a godsend. It seems to work well, because (unlike?) our old method, we are giving them no time to get foolish in, and they sit in like little majors ... Practice has all gone to hell this week. I am grubbing at some stuff for a Shaks(peare) Club on Friday ... and the scarlet paper under it all. And the Medicine and Pathology Sections for Toronto to write. Tell us the title of your papers ... The Medical Dinner was a great drunk: the worst in years. Timed for 8:30, began at 9:40, all full of cocktails, of course speeches inaudible. (January 1910)

Your letter received. It was a --- of a poor letter ... Likewise the paper came ok, and is in the chief's (Adami's) hands. After he pulls its guts out, I will do as you suggest and skip it. What a --- of a stale thing is life! I've got enough work to keep me out of mischief and it 'worrits' me. Bill's (Turner) idea is that we both need loosening up. I have so damned many things on my soul at present that I can't sit down and be ordinarily gay without my conscience say "my dear fellow, art is long and time is fleeting, and you ought to be doing this and that.'

Drinking seems to have fallen away since you left: I personally have lost my taste for 'licker' and Billy (Turner) and Harry (?) are far from being well-men (or tap men either). (February 1910)

Busy as hell! A lull in PMs the last week, but by Febs end we were about 38 or 48. The chief does the microscopic work because I'm so --- busy with the wards and the practice that I can't get the time.

The Virgins and the Bull Pen are all well: but Windy Bill (Turner) complains that he needs loosening up, and I feel the same way myself. So --- busy, I don't know which way to turn.

I hope you are getting a chair of Drink established at Pittsburgh. (March 1910)[7]

In about 1908 McCrae went to live in the house of Dr Edward Archibald, occupying a top floor apartment separate from that of the family. He remained there until 1914. Archibald was one of the outstanding figures of his generation in Canadian medicine. The same age as McCrae, he was born in Montreal and graduated from McGill in medicine in 1896, having done some of his studies in France. After working as a resident at the Royal Victoria Hospital, he then studied pathology and surgery in Germany for one year before returning to the surgical staff of the Royal Victoria. He developed pulmonary tuberculosis in 1901 but recovered after a year at Saranac Lake. He was to become a skilled and innovative thoracic surgeon. Archibald was another of McCrae's friends whose qualities of character seem inadequately described by superlatives. One of McCrae's interns later made a curious comment about McCrae's life in Archibald's house. He noted that there were "not many households in which the experiment could have been made to work, especially with a man like McCrae. But their ... years of peaceful life is comment enough on the relationship."[8] Archibald shared with McCrae a passion for his profession, integrity, and an interest in reading and in history. McCrae was greatly attached to the Archibald children.

Despite his busy life, McCrae was still popular and found time for people. Friends included fellow physicians from the Royal Victoria Hospital — the surgeon L.L. Reford, the gynaecologist W.W. Chipman, the physician J.C. Meakin, and friends from the medical faculty, Campbell Palmer Howard and the chemist R.F. Ruttan. A great friend was W.T. (Billy) Turner, with whom he sometimes took holidays in Europe. Some of these men later worked with McCrae in France. The English-speaking community in Montreal seems to have mixed little with the French-speaking community.

McCrae was a member of a Shakespearean Club, the University Club, the Military Institute Club of Montreal, the *Zeta Psi* fraternity, and St Paul's Presbyterian Church. His leisure was spent in pursuits associated with these bodies, in reading, and in travel. He was a member of a select group who belonged to the Pen and Pencil Club, which met fortnightly in the studio of the artist Edouard Dyonnet. Andrew Macphail, with his gorgeous sense of being one of the elect, described it as a "peculiar club. It contained no member who should not be in it; and no one was left out who should be in."[9] It was a drinking club which, as Leacock said, "permitted (with some reluctance) its members to read it their literary efforts."[10] Other members included artists, writers, and teachers. It was to them that McCrae read his poetry.

McCrae published five poems between the years 1906 and 1910, all in his friend Macphail's *University Magazine*. Three were about death or grief, four had military themes, and two were about courage. They had lost much of the gloominess of his earlier poetry.

The unconquered dead was published in 1906, inspired by a visit to the battlefield of Magersfontein in South Africa, where General Methuen had been defeated in late 1899. It is a poem that foreshadows *In Flanders Fields*.

The unconquered dead

...defeated, with great loss.

Not we the conquered! Not to us the blame
    Of them that flee, of them that basely yield;
    Nor ours the shout of victory, the fame
Of them that vanquish in a stricken field.

That day of battle in the dusty heat
    We lay and heard the bullets swish and sing
Like scythes amid the over-ripened wheat,
    And we the harvest of their garnering.

Some yielded, No, not we! Not we, we swear
  By these our wounds; this trench upon the hill
Where all the shell-strewn earth is seamed and bare.
  Was ours to keep; and lo! we have it still.

We might have yielded, even we, but death
  Came for our helper; like a sudden flood
The crashing darkness fell; our painful breath
  We drew with gasps amid the choking blood.

The roar fell faint and further off, and soon
  Sank to a foolish humming in our ears,
Like crickets in the long, hot afternoon
  Among the wheat fields of the olden years.

Before our eyes a boundless wall of red
  Shot through by sudden streaks of jagged pain!
Then a slow-gathering darkness overhead
  And rest came on us like a quiet rain.

Not we the conquered! Not to us the shame,
  Who hold our earthen ramparts, nor shall cease
To hold them ever; victors we, who came
  In that fierce moment to our honoured peace.

University Magazine, 1906

Two poems were published in 1907 in the *University Magazine*. One, *The oldest drama*, may have been inspired by a sermon and deals with the characteristic McCrae themes of grief and death, but it also has a leavening of pity. The other poem, *The warrior*, was said to have been inspired by a poor, physically handicapped patient of his.

The oldest drama

"It fell on a day, that he went out to his father to the reapers. And he said unto his father, My head, my head. And he said to a lad, Carry him to his mother. And ... he sat on her knees till noon, and then died. And she went up, and laid him on the bed ... And shut the door upon him and went out."

Immortal story that no mother's heart
  Ev'n yet can read, nor feel the biting pain
That rent her soul! Immortal not by art
  Which makes a long past sorrow sting again

56

Like grief of yesterday: but since it said
    In simplest word the truth which all may see,
Where any mother sobs above her dead
    And plays anew the silent tragedy.

University Magazine, 1907

The warrior

He wrought in poverty, the dull grey days,
    But with the night his little lamp-lit room
Was bright with battle flame, or through a haze
    Of smoke that stung his eyes he heard the boom
Of Blucher's guns; he shared Almeida's scars,
    And from the close-packed deck, about to die,
Looked up and saw the *Birkenhead's* tall spars
    Weave wavering lines across the Southern sky:

Or in the stifling 'tween decks, row on row
    At Aboukir, saw how the dead men lay;
Charged with the fiercest in Busaco's strife,
Brave dreams are his — the flick-ring lamp burns low —
Yet couraged for the battles of the day
    He goes to stand full face to face with life.

University Magazine, 1907

What is probably his finest poem, *Isandlwana*, was published in 1910. It originated from a visit to the town of Brecon in Wales, where he met a deranged middle-aged woman whose son had been killed at the massacre by Zulus of 2,500 British soldiers in 1879. The battle was the most crushing defeat for the British army since the first Afghan War.

Isandlwana

Scarlet coats, and crash o' the band,
    The grey of a pauper's gown,
    A soldier's grave in Zululand,
And a woman in Brecon Town.

My little lad for a soldier boy,
    (Mother's o' Brecon Town!)
My eyes for tears and his for joy
    When he went from Brecon Town,

His for the flags and the gallants sights
His for the medals and his for the fights,
And mine for the dreary, rainy nights
    At home in Brecon Town.

They say he's laid beneath a tree,
    (Come back to Brecon Town!)
Shouldn't I know? — I was there to see:
    (It's far to Brecon Town!)
It's me that keeps it trim and drest
With a briar there and a rose by his breast —
The English flowers he likes the best
    That I bring from Brecon Town.

And I sit beside him — him and me,
    (We're back to Brecon Town.)
To talk of the things that used to be
    (Grey ghosts of Brecon Town);
I know the look o' the land and sky,
And the bird that builds in the tree near by,
And times I hear the jackals cry,
    And me in Brecon Town.

Golden grey on miles of sand
    The dawn comes creeping down;
It's day in far off Zululand
        And night in Brecon Town.

University Magazine, 1910

CHAPTER EIGHT
JOHN McCRAE AND THE EMPIRE

Three friends of McCrae from the Pen and Pencil Club and the university — Macphail, Leacock, and John Macnaughton — were influential Canadian imperialists, and the circle in which McCrae moved in Montreal was one which held imperialist ideas. Canadian imperialism, as historian Carl Berger has argued, was a form of Canadian nationalism, a native product embedded in the traditions of the country. It was a reaction to colonialism; Leacock said, "I am an Imperialist because I will not be a Colonial."[1] It was a movement that pushed for closer union of the empire, in an economic, political, and military sense, as a means of giving Canada influence over imperial policy. Imperialists emphasized a respect for history, the importance of community over the individual, a distrust of materialism, and the importance of religion. It was felt that at times Canadian interests had been sacrificed to Britain. Imperialists wanted an equal share in the empire, and hoped that Canada would become the empire's centre.

Canada, these men thought, was caught between two imperialisms, that of Britain and of the United States. The latter would result in the annihilation of Canada's national identity, but within the empire the nation could develop and eventually gain prominence. The British constitution was seen as superior to that of the United States, and Canada was progressing without the social instability, violence, and lawlessness of American society. Immigration into the United States by southern and eastern Europeans in the late 19th century was diluting the Anglo-Saxon strain and resulting in the violence and corruption of American politics and institutions. As for Canada, the enormous expansion of the population and of the economy at the turn of the century gave rise to renewed hope in the country's future as a nation independent of the United States. Successful Canadian participation in the Boer War reflected increasing maturity and was a further step on the road to nationhood.

For Canadian imperialists, the British empire had a divine mission to Christianize and civilize the world, and was under an obligation to carry out the will of God. The British mission was to extend the ideas of freedom, justice, and peace to the races under its protection. The empire was not an opportunity for a scramble for power or wealth, but for idealistic service, for duty, and for self-sacrifice in carrying out God's will for the world. The end of the empire was ultimately spiritual. Some of the imperialists' ideas were those of Carlyle — the idea that the human will, inspired by ideals, could change history, and the idea of work as a virtue in itself which resulted in progress. Imperialists, as well, relied on Darwinism to support their view that mankind was subject to the evolutionary forces at play in nature, but they also argued that these forces

Sir Andrew Macphail, from a portrait. (Public Archives of Prince Edward Island, 2320, 2-12)

were not random and blind but were under control of a creative agent. History was not accident; it was a story of progress as man bowed to the divine will. It was certainly not accident which placed one-quarter of the world under the empire's protection. The rapid and dramatic progress in all fields, including that of medicine, seen in Queen Victoria's lifetime reinforced the sense that the empire was doing something right.

Imperialism and national military preparedness were closely linked, and were bridged by militarism. "War was an inevitable form of the universal struggle for existence"[2] and a "necessary incident in social evolution" rather than a minor aberration in the acquisition of empire. The soldierly character, with its ideas of service and self-sacrifice, duty and obedience, provided an antidote to the dilemmas of contemporary life, which was characterized by a distasteful struggle for material advantage and power. Military preparedness and self-defence were also important as indicators of self-reliant nationhood. In 1907 Lord Strathcona gave four million dollars to encourage military and physical training in schools, a justification being that "we need the military virtues more against ourselves than against any possible external foe"[3] in order to prevent the moral and physical degeneration of the race. John McCrae's father gave money for gymnasium equipment at the Ontario Agricultural College for the same reason.

Imperialists were conservative. Their ideas were those of the Victorian prophets and were influenced by the new evolutionary science. They did not adulate Britain, which was often even thought of as degenerate. The white colonies, and particularly Canada, were thought to have taken the best from the mother country, left the worst behind, and, under the stimulating climatic influences and tests of the struggling pioneer days, to have won the position of leadership that once belonged to the mother country. McCrae talked to the Women's Canadian Club of Hamilton about Canadian traditions and deplored the neglect of Canadian history in the schools, saying: "Canadians should be guided by the traditions of their forefathers and not become drones in the hive of the British Empire."[4] This speech was not anti-British but was in the imperialistic mould; the key word was "drones."

Many of the imperialists' ideas — the obligations of history, fulfilling God's will through work, self-sacrifice, obedience, the importance of military values, the idea that life's aims were spiritual and not materialistic, and that life was a schoolground and not as playground — were those of John McCrae. The assumptions of the age were subscribed to by those leaders of Canadian life who lived in Montreal around the turn of the century.

Andrew Macphail, McCrae's friend and his biographer, was born in Prince Edward Island in 1864. He financed his early university education by teaching in a one-room school house from the age of 18 and later supported himself through medical studies at McGill by journalism, graduating in 1891. He was pathologist at the Western Hospital and Verdun Hospital from 1895 to 1906, when he became professor of the history of medicine at McGill. He was knighted in 1918 for his war service with the Field Ambulance. He became the foremost literary figure of his generation in Canada, saying that it was "the library that destroyed me; Matthew Arnold, Ruskin, Walter Pater, Walter Bagehot, Renan and Saint Beuve must bear the chief blame." In 1893 he married a wealthy heiress, who died in 1902 leaving him with two children. He never remarried. In collaboration with McCrae he collected all the poems on bereavement and sorrow he could find; these poems, though initially collected for his own use, were eventually published in 1916 as *The book of sorrow*, a 500-page effort which included McCrae's *Isandlwana* and *Cometh the night*.

Macphail carried a perpetual air of gloom and deliberation. He had an inquiring intellect and a dry Scottish humour which was, as Leacock described, "of that truly Scottish kind which is best when least shared." He loved epigrams and mystification. In 1907 he became the editor of the quarterly *University Magazine*, which was formed from the old *McGill University Magazine* and supported by the universities of McGill, Dalhousie, and Toronto. There was a board of directors (including McCrae) but "after a meeting or two the magazine became and remained Andrew Macphail."[5] It was devoted to politics and literature and was influential, although its circulation was not large. Partly financed out of Macphail's pocket, it was a vehicle of imperialist thought.

Macphail was convinced that whiteness was the highest rank on the evolutionary scale, and the peculiar blending of the English genes had given rise to the genius of the English nation. For him the English system of government, based on conservative principles and on an aristocracy to which many could rise by work, discipline, and development of moral character of moral character, was ideal. He was suspicious of democracy, following Carlyle in his axiom that "England never was a democracy, is not now, and never will be until England is not England." For him imperialism was an intangible experience, a way of looking at things, the birthright of the British people, a loyalty to the past. He shared the imperialist belief that the pursuit of wealth and power were morally damaging; service and self-sacrifice were more important. John McCrae was a man after his own heart.

Stephen Leacock, the well-known writer of humorous stories and a lecturer in political economy at McGill, was another of McCrae's friends in Montreal. The son of an alcoholic English gentleman, he was educated at Upper Canada College and the University of Toronto, where he was in the same fraternity and the same militia company as McCrae. He taught for 10 years at Upper Canada College under the headmaster John Parkin, secretary of the Imperial Federation League and later of the Rhodes Trust. Leacock was persuaded by Lord Grey, the governor general, to make a tour of the empire in 1907, lecturing on "Imperial Development and Organization." He was a Canadian patriot and an eloquent and devoted apologist for the British empire, writing often on the theme for Macphail's *University Magazine*. A bluff, arrogant, reticent, careless, and masculine man, he enjoyed whisky and male company. He was torn by the conflicts in late Victorian life and criticized its class distinctions and the complacency over poverty, but he was pulled between wanting economic and social justice for citizens and his distrust of political schemes, especially socialist, which might reform society but erode individual liberties. Like Macphail, he feared that the destruction of Victorian values in the 19th century meant the destruction of all values. A man who wrote about the dangers of surrender to materialist values, he was himself a materialist. He saw Canada as a bridge between the two great white nations of Britain and the United States, and wrote often in support of the ideas of imperial federation and Greater Britain; although heavily in favour of protectionism in trade between Canada and the United States, he was not anti-American.

A third friend of McCrae's from the Pen and Pencil Club was John Macnaughton. Born in Scotland in 1858, he was ordained a minister of the Presbyterian Church and taught Greek and Latin at Queen's University in Kingston from 1899. He later taught at McGill from 1908. Macnaughton was a man of great vitality, an eccentric with outspoken views on many subjects. He hated prohibition, disliked Americans, was anti-proletarian, and was an admirer of Thomas Carlyle and of Principal George Grant of Queen's, a leading imperialist.

In contrast to his three friends, McCrae wrote nothing on imperialism. His attitude is best described in the McGill Memorial Service address in early 1918, given by John Macnaughton:

> He came back, too, just as good a Canadian as he had been when he set out (for South Africa), but certainly ... much more of a Britisher than ever he had been before. He came home an Imperialist. In the ears of a many good sort of people the word has a sinister sound. It suggests the brutal insolence of national pride and agrandisement, the instinct of domination over the races. There is really very little danger of that under our institutions, he thought. British Imperialism (is) a very mild reality under a rather clumsily aggressive name. For it simply means that the British people believe in the value of their birthright, which they take to be ... identical with the maintenance of freedom and decency in the world, and are, therefore, prepared to face the responsibilities that birthright implies, and give up their lives, if need be, rather than be false to them. With John McCrae, too, as with most simple men, it meant a deep instinctive loyalty to the past, the call of the blood, the sacred claims of the old cradle of our race, the home of our ideals.[6]

* * *

In August 1910 the Governor General of Canada from 1904 to 1911, Lord Grey, made an expedition from Norway House on Lake Winnipeg to Hudson Bay, along the river route of the old Hudson's Bay Company to the Canadian northwest. The prairie provinces wanted a port on the west of Hudson Bay which could be reached by rail from Winnipeg. They argued that, because of the curvature of the earth, Hudson Bay was as near Liverpool as Montreal, and that such a port might break the economic grip of eastern Canada on the west.

Hudson Bay trip with Earl Grey, 1910. First campfire. Flag floating over His Excellency Earl Grey's quarters. (Public Archives of Canada, PA 45252)

Hudson Bay trip with Earl Grey, 1910. Kyack being inspected by His Excellency Earl Grey at Churchill, Manitoba. John McCrae and John Macnaughton look on. (Public Archives of Canada, PA 45198)

On the trip were Lord Grey, his cousin, his ADC, the director of the Geological Survey, John Macnaughton, Leo Amery of the London *Times*, and McCrae, who went as the expedition's doctor. They took one dozen canoes, paddled by two dozen hymn-singing Methodist Cree Indians. McCrae shared a canoe and tent with Amery. The river journey took eleven days to York Factory, where they were picked up by steamer and went, via Labrador, past Newfoundland. They did not visit Newfoundland because of the danger of inciting rumours of annexation of the colony by Canada. But they did call in at New Brunswick. Nova Scotia and Cape Breton; they also stayed in Prince Edward Island with Andrew Macphail. Finally they travelled up the St Lawrence to Quebec. The entire journey took two months. McCrae was the life of the party. Grey later said that "we travelled 3,000 miles and McCrae had a different story for every one of them,"[4] and Amery wrote that "as a story teller he never met his equal, every night in the tent or at the campfire he poured out anecdotes, never repeated."[5]

McCrae was a friend of Lord Grey; during the Great War Grey wrote to McCrae regularly. The son of the private secretary to Prince Albert, and later to Queen Victoria, Grey was described later by John Macnaughton as a "jolly, brave English boy," and his one overwhelming enthusiasm was the empire. In his youth he became interested in social reform and "saw in (British) domestic poverty and wretchedness as deep a national and a human shame as, in a national development of the British Empire, he saw a remedy for all our home ills and a future of quite boundless magnificence for the entire family of man."[9] Grey entered Parliament as a Liberal but broke with Gladstone over the first Home Rule Bill. He had a spiritual conception of empire — "altogether above the sordid economic covetousness of Caesarian arrogance of the professional jingo, his spirit soared towards its vision of the future."[10] Like a good English aristocrat,

He loved a good woman; he loved a good horse. But there was never beautiful woman nor beautiful horse in all this wide world could compare in his eyes with the beauty of the British Empire. It was to him the magic beauty of the world. He never had any jingo feeling about it.... Under the British flag, wherever he journeyed, he found men of English speech living in an atmosphere of liberty and carrying on the dear domestic traditions of the British Isles. He saw justice firmly planted there, industry and invention unfettered by tyrants of any kind, and our old English kindness and cheerfulness and broadminded tolerance keeping things together.... The Empire wasn't a word to him. It was a vast, almost boundless home for honest men. He had seen with his own eyes its great prairies and veldts, its forests and jungles, its lakes and rivers, its mountains and valleys, its endless leagues of unhandtilled land waiting for the plough.... He knew that so long as Britons keep the ancient faith of their fathers the extension of their rule must work for the benefit of mankind.[11]

After the abortive Jameson Raid in South Africa, Grey was for a time chairman of Cecil Rhodes' Chartered Company and a great admirer of that unscrupulous man, though he must have been perplexed by him more than once. Lord Milner wrote: "Grey, excellent, simple-minded fellow, would not be one-tenth the use he undoubtedly is, if he did not take Rhodes at his own valuation."[12]

Grey wanted a federal structure for the empire, a federal parliament in London, and he saw the London War Conferences of the Dominion Ministers as a shadow of the future scheme. He was frustrated by the lack of awareness of the empire in England, by the inability of the English to "think Imperially," but hoped that a new imperial structure might solve the many social problems plaguing England. "There is no need of poverty and overcrowding (in England) if we make intelligent use of the Empire."[13] Like Kipling, he was prepared for an Anglo-Saxon union of Britain and the United States, but he nevertheless believed that to England "more than any other country, it seems to me that the fortunes of God are committed. Therefore it is her bounden duty to live for the highest causes of humanity."[14]

Another on the journey, Leo S. Amery, was a more complex man, with a pragmatic rather than religious approach to the problems of imperialism. Born in 1873, he was a contemporary at Harrow of Winston Churchill. His early thinking was shaped by Seeley's *Expansion of England* and by hearing John Parkin, the head of Upper Canada College, talk on imperial federation. He was educated at Balliol and later became a Fellow of All Souls, where he continued his interest in imperial unity. In 1899 he joined the *Times* and was for a short while correspondent in Germany. There he became aware of the "deep-seated hostility of the German people, of its hopes of forcibly displacing the English from their place in the sun."[15] Amery became the *Times* correspondent in South Africa; it was during his time there as a guest of Amery that Kipling met McCrae in 1900. Amery spent many years after the Boer War editing and writing *The Times history of the South African war*, which he used heavily to criticize the conduct and organisation of the British army and in which he urged reform based on the South African experiences to "regenerate an effete military and political system in light of the lessons."[16] Amery pleaded for National Service, a compulsory military training for all Englishmen like that seen in Europe, and he started the National Service League because of fear of war with Germany. He was opposed to free trade and advocated instead imperial preferential tariffs to strengthen the industrial base of Britain, in part because he knew what the *Zollverein* had done for German unity. Amery worked hard to promote imperial unity, emphasizing the principle of equal partnership of the white colonies with the mother country, a partnership in which the colonies would have influence over imperial foreign policy. Like many English imperialists, he was afraid that the white colonies would grow to full nationhood and leave the mother country with the bitter legacies of the industrial revolution and with an economic base no longer competitive with rivals such as the United States and Germany.

Everything John McCrae did and thought had the hallmarks of Canadian imperialism: his participation in the Boer War, his sense of history, his nationalism, his anti-materialism, his militarism, his friendships with staunch imperialists, and his behaviour at the start of the Great War. McCrae's imperialism was, in part, based on nationalistic pride, and in part, as Macnaughton wrote, on his belief in the British people's duty to maintain justice in the world.

John McCrae in 1912. (McCrae Birthplace Museum)

CHAPTER NINE
LAST YEARS IN MONTREAL: 1911-14

By 1911 McCrae was one of the more senior and respected teachers and physicians in Montreal. He was busy because of the demand for his skills and because of his methods of work. Dr Sclater Lewis, an intern at the Royal Victoria Hospital in 1912, described how "McCrae liked to maintain a more personal contact with patients, did not delegate authority, and as a result received many night calls from members of his staff.... Accurate case records were insisted on."[1] The pressure of work at times exacerbated McCrae's temper. He wrote Klotz in March 1911: "Ordinarily, I keep (my temper) down, and only break occasionally. To --- much work."[2] One story goes that McCrae insisted on washing his hands between wards, and that the head nurse had to turn on the taps and hold out the towel. On one occasion the head nurse forgot to turn on the cold tap — McCrae in the middle of one of his myriad stories, paid no attention and plunged his hands into the scalding water. He struggled with rage — but instead of the expected outburst quoted from the Book of Proverbs, "and he who guardeth his spirit is better than he who takes a strong city."[3]

Between 1909 and 1911 McCrae wrote a textbook with Adami, based on the latter's *Principles of pathology* which was highly successful among professional pathologists but unsuitable for students. Adami proposed that McCrae help him to write a student version. It involved McCrae in an immense amount of editorial work, which he finished in December 1911. The book was published in 1912 as A *textbook of pathology for students of medicine*. It sold well, and a second edition was prepared in 1914.

Between 1911 and 1914 McCrae wrote scientific abstracts for the *American Journal of Medical Science*, a journal edited by Oskar Klotz. The subjects he covered included Wasserman's therapy for cancer; the possibility that Landsteiner and Levadiditi had discovered a viral cause for scarlet fever; vaccination; paleopathology; antityphoid serum; the detection of horseflesh in sausages; the therapy of syphilis with salvarsan; the life cycles of the glanders and pseudo-tuberculosis bacilli in man; and many other diverse subjects, often gleaned from the German and French literature.

McCrae was at times urged to leave McGill and find a better appointment elsewhere. He wrote to Klotz in 1911: "The idea of 'up and out' rather daunts me. Rhea was offered the chance of Harvard, but is staying and has been made Assistant Professor."[4] And in 1912 he wrote that "Burgess, the new Pathologist at the General seems a decent chap: though young, he is married, and I suppose they expect to keep him longer on that account."

McCrae never married, though he was attractive to many women. Some of the reasons for his not marrying were traced in letters to Klotz in which he describes his romance with "Lady S.R."

January 1910: "The Lady R. is going to New York tomorrow or the next day, leaving me a choice between suicide and work."

January 1910: "I miss my wife sadly: I hope she doesn't like the heat too well — so meantime, I have cut girling out of my time-table."

March 1910: "The lady seems to be getting much too satisfied with her lot in New York."

December 1910: "S.R. my wife is here at present ... but I see her only at intervals. I would gladly make a journey down to see you, and bring her but it might cost you your place in the College."

June 1911: "My wife came to town Sunday and says she is going to marry somebody or other in the fall."

December 1912: "The bride writes me occasionally from Vancouver to tell me how happy she is. John Todd married in Paris. Among all these marryings and givings in marriage you will wonder that 160 (Metcalfe Street) has nothing doing."

March 1913: "Lady R. writes ... she is not yet divorced. Everything quiet here except for work. Life does not contain much fun."

February 1914: "I am sober and very virtuous."[5]

The struggles of his early professional life left him little time or money for thoughts of marriage; following Osler's advice he "put his emotions on ice" and put his energy into establishing a professional reputation. He treated women with charm and courtesy, and several hoped to marry him. There are stories that in 1914 he became secretly engaged to Nona Gwyn, the sister of Tom McCrae's wife, from Dundas, Ontario. She was favourite niece of William Osler in whose Oxford house she lived in 1910. Osler described her as "plain but very sweet; our style." Following John McCrae's death Nona claimed to have been engaged to him and showed a ring to prove it. She also said that the engagement was broken off in 1917. He was so charming and was such a hero to his generation that several women came forward after his death to say that they had been engaged to him.

Although McCrae worked hard at his university teaching and at his increasingly busy practice, the advantage of working in a university was that he could take time off. He holidayed at various times in England, France, and Europe, sometimes with his friend and fellow bachelor Dr Billy Turner. At times he worked his passage to Europe as ship's surgeon; he enjoyed ships and the sea. These were the compensations of a bachelor life.

McCrae regularly attended the Presbyterian Sunday morning services at St Paul's Church throughout his Montreal period. His Sunday afternoons were spent visiting patients. His religious faith remained strong and was described by his friend John Macnaughton as that of the "simplest faith of childhood ... By nature (he was) so sure about the main things ... of which all formulated faiths are but a more or less stammering expression ... his instinctive faith sufficed him ... And, indeed, his life was so active otherwise, his mind so completely absorbed in the richer spectacle of full-bodied life."[6]

McCrae's faith is present in his post-1900 poetry, including *The dead master*, written on the death of a musician in Montreal in 1913.

> Amid earth's vagrant noises, he caught
>   the note sublime:
>
> To-day around him surges from the
>   silences of Time
>
> A flood of nobler music, like a river deep and
>   broad,
>
> Fit song for heroes gathered in the banquet-
>   hall of God.

University Magazine, 1913

In 1913 McCrae also wrote *Cometh the night*, a poem that again dealt with the theme of death as the end to human endeavour, a theme he had not used for some years

> Cometh the night. The wind falls low,
>   The trees swing slowly to and fro:
>   Around the church the headstones grey
>   Cluster, like children strayed away
> But found again, and folded so.
>
> No chiding look doth she bestow:
> If she is glad, they cannot know;
>   If ill or well they spend their day,
>   Cometh the night.
>
> Singing or sad, intent they go;
> They do not see the shadow grow;
>   There yet is time, they lightly say,
>   Before our work aside we lay;
>   Their task is but half-done, and lo
>   Cometh the night.

University Magazine, 1913

In August 1913 the 17th International Medical Congress was held in London and attended by Osler and many from McGill, including McCrae. It

John McCrae enjoying a favourite relaxation. (McCrae Birthplace Museum)

was just 30 years since the conference had heard the remarkable discoveries of Pasteur, Lister, Virchow, and Koch. One of the highlights at the 1913 conference was a dinner given by the 93-year-old Canadian high commissioner in London, Lord Strathcona, for the 1,300 participants. He insisted on shaking hands with all his guests until Osler distracted his attention. It was said after Strathcona's death in 1914 that "British Imperialism was largely the joint product of four men — Joseph Chamberlain, Lord Strathcona, Rudyard Kipling, and Lord Northcliffe." The history of modern Canada was in part the history of Lord Strathcona — a governor of the Hudson Bay Company, a prisoner of Louis Riel in the Red River Rebellion, the man who with the Canadian Pacific Railway saved much of Canada from American annexation, who equipped Strathcona's Horse for South Africa, and who encouraged British immigration. He did much for medicine in Montreal. As a young man he had himself wanted to become a physician but had been too poor to afford it.

In 1913 McCrae wrote *The captain* about the naming of a modern battleship after an earlier fighting ship. War clouds were on the horizon, and in two years McCrae was to be fighting at the battle of Ypres.

> *Here all the day she swings from tide to tide,*
> *Here all night long she tugs a rusted chain*
> *A masterless hulk that was a ship of pride,*
> *Yet unashamed: her memories remain.*

It was Nelson in the *Captain*, Cape St. Vincent far alee,
    With the *Vanguard* leading s'uth'ard in the haze —
Little Jervis and the Spaniards and the fight that was to be,
Twenty-seven Spanish battleships, great bullies of the sea,
    And the *Captain* there to find her day of days.

Right into them the *Vanguard* leads, but with a sudden tack
    The Spaniards double swiftly on their trail;
Now Jervis overshoots his mark, like some too eager pack,
He will not overtake them, haste he e'er so greatly back,
    But Nelson and the *Captain* will not fail.

Like a tigress on her quarry leaps the *Captain* from her place,
    To lie across the fleeing squadron's way:
Heavy odds and heavy onslaught, gun to gun and face to face,
Win the ship a name of glory, win the men a death of grace,
    For a little hold the Spanish fleet in play.

Ended now the *Captain*'s battle, stricken wore she falls aside
    Holding still her foemen, beaten to the knee:
As the *Vanguard* drifted past her, Well done, *Captain*, Jervis cried,
Rang the cheers of men that conquered, ran the blood of men that died
    And the ship had won her immortality.

> *Lo! here her progeny of steel and steam,*
> *A funnelled monster at her mooring swings:*
> *Still, in our hearts, we see her pennant stream,*
> *And Well done, Captain, like a trumpet rings.*

University Magazine, 1913

In 1914 a second edition of Adami's and McCrae's textbook was prepared; McCrae finished the editing in Atlantic City and on 29 July left for England by ship, "for better or worse, with the world so disturbed I would gladly have stayed more in touch with events, but I dare say one is just as happy away from the hundred conflicting reports."[7] Nearing England on 5 August, he wrote: "All is excitement; the ship runs without lights. Surely the German Kaiser has his head in the noose at last: it will be a terrible war, and the finish of one or the other. I am afraid my holiday trip is knocked galley west; but we shall see."[8]

Once war had broken out, McCrae felt that he could not return home. He cabled his old friend from South Africa, E.W.B. Morrison, the Director of Artillery, Permanent Force, in Ottawa to inform him that he was available as a "combatant or medical if they need me," and waited impatiently for the reply. "If they want me for the Canadian forces," he said, "I could use my old Sam Browne belt, sword and saddle if it is yet extant. At times I wish I could go home with a clear conscience."[10]

McCrae was provisionally offered the appointment of brigade surgeon by Morrison, and sailed home at the end of August.

CLC Allinson, England, 1915. (Courtesy of Mrs. C. Macleod)

74

CHAPTER TEN
THE FIRST CANADIAN EXPEDITIONARY
FORCE: NEUVE CHAPELLE

The origins of the First World War are complex. Liddell Hart wrote that "fifty years were spent in the process of making Europe explosive." The presence of large armies and navies for the protection and exploitation of their empires by the English, French, Russians, and Austro-Hungarians made up the gunpowder which was ignited by the growth of the German Reich and its lust for "a place in the sun." The large armies of the imperial powers led to the militarization of their societies which was enhanced by current social interpretations of the evolutionary theory of Darwin. These interpretations regarded war as a biological necessity and nations as becoming great from a struggle for the "survival of the fittest."

The British felt threatened by the growth of German trade and influence, by the hostility of Germany over the Boer war, and by the rapid growth of the German navy. The French wanted revenge for the humiliations of the 1870 Franco-Prussian war. The German Kaiser's bellicose attitude from 1900 onwards spread alarm and distrust in the other European powers and was a chief cause of the war. The Kaiser sought his way by threats and many countries feared the mailed fist of Germany. Because of the impending clash of imperialisms Europe became a complex mixture of interlocking treaties between the great powers which almost guaranteed general war should any country attack another. As Britain moved from her isolationist stance to alliance with France and Russia, in response to German threats, Germany in turn felt encircled by potential enemies and became increasingly paranoid. Within Germany and Russia the militarists saw war as a safety valve for the developing social unrest.

In England the years that led up to the Great War were years of deep social unrest. The Edwardian garden-party, with its clink of glasses and crack of croquet mallets, hid a turmoil in the house and in the village. A threat of a general strike in 1914 promised revolution, the revolt in Ireland threatened a civil war, and the suffragettes made a mockery of the traditional political *status quo*. The English public "was only aware of an inner tension, a need for stimulants; and what could be more exciting than to gather together all the political rages, all the class hatreds, all the fevers for spending and excitement and speed, which then seemed to hang like a haunted fog over England — to gather them and condense them thus into one huge shape and call it Germany?" The English "public in 1914 resembled a man who is approaching a nervous breakdown ... it is not hard to see why the country should have found in the outbreak of war ... something like deliverance and fulfillment."[1]

The outbreak of war between Britain and Germany was precipitated by the German invasion of neutral Belgium. Unlike England, Canada was not a country on the verge of a nervous breakdown, but there was widespread and enthusiastic support in English Canada for the war. Macphail wrote in the *Canadian Medical Association Journal*: "It is enough for us that the Empire which is our heritage, is involved in a struggle for self preservation, and on the side of the weak against the strong, of international justice against brutalizing militarism."[2] Duty called men to the fight.

Canada declared war on Germany on 4 August, one day after the British Parliament had done so. Prime Minister Robert Borden stated, "our recognition of this war as ours ... determines absolutely once and for all that we have passed from the status of the protected colony to that of the participating nation." Recruiting in Canada was stopped at the end of August, since 45,000 volunteers had joined up in three weeks, and Great Britain had suggested that Canada's contribution be what was then thought to be the enormous contribution of one division of 22,000 men.

Minister of Defence Sam Hughes precipitated chaos by ignoring his department's mobilization scheme and appealing for volunteers directly rather than using the existing militia regiments. To the bitterness of the militia he abolished the regimental units and started the numbered battalions of the Canadian Expeditionary Force. Hughes assembled the volunteers at Valcartier, near Quebec City, a bare piece of ground swiftly transformed into a camp for 32,000 men and 8,000 horses ruled over by his despotic self. The First Canadian Division consisted of three infantry brigades. The First Brigade of Canadian Field Artillery was commanded by Lt. Col. E.W.B. Morrison, McCrae's friend from South Africa. Morrison had been the editor of the Ottawa *Citizen*, but in 1913 he had joined the Permanent Force (the Canadian regular army and navy, consisting of 3,300 men) as director of artillery in the Department of Militia and Defence Headquarters. His brigade was made up of four batteries and a headquarter staff of the adjutant, Lt. Col. W.O.H. Dodds, Orderly Officer L.V.M. Cosgrave, and chaplains (including Canon Almond, a friend of McCrae from South Africa and later Montreal). Morrison wanted McCrae to be a lieutenant-colonel and have command of his own artillery brigade, but since this was not possible (on account of his age, 41, and his lack of recent artillery experience) McCrae was made brigade-surgeon, with the rank of Major, and second-in-command of the brigade. McCrae never wore the Red Cross armband of a non-combatant medical officer; photographs of the period show him with revolver and sword. A close friend of Captain Cosgrave was a lieutenant in the 2nd Battery, Alexis Helmer, a graduate of McGill and the Royal Military College, who also became a friend of McCrae. C.L.C. Allinson was general duty corporal in the headquarters staff; he later wrote an unpublished manuscript about McCrae.

McCrae returned to Canada in early September 1914. He did not go to Guelph judging that his visit would be too harrowing for his mother. He wrote to his sister, Geills:

Out on the awful old trail again! And with very mixed feelings, but some determination.... We can hope for happier times. Everyone most kind and helpful: my going does not seem to surprise anyone ... I am in good hope of coming back soon and safely: that, I am glad to say, is in other and better hands than ours.[3]

He called in at Montreal and dined with Macphail in the University Club, where he was aglow with enthusiasm for his new adventure. His friend John Todd gave him a present of a horse, Bonfire, to whom he became deeply attached. Just before leaving Canada, McCrae wrote to a woman friend:

It is a terrible state of affairs, and I am going because I think every bachelor, especially if he has experience of war, ought to go. I am really rather afraid, but more afraid to stay at home with my conscience.... we have fifty-four (18-pounder) field guns in three Brigades, besides heavier guns — perfectly equipped.[4]

Canadian Artillery loading a field gun, World War I. (Public Archives of Canada, PA 22712)

On 3 October the First Contingent left the Gaspé Basin to cheering crowds. The contingent consisted of 1,424 officers, 29,197 men of other ranks, 7,000 horses, and motor and wagon transport — all boarded on 33 ships. Of the men, nearly two-thirds were born in the British Isles, but over two-thirds of the officers were Canadian-born and militia-trained. The force expected to land in France and go soon into the fighting, but they were not required since the Germans had been halted on the Marne. The division landed at Plymouth to a rapturous reception and within a few days was on Salisbury Plain in southern England, where the men camped in four areas.

Whatever its enthusiasm, the contingent was poorly trained. It was described by one of the British General Staff as "a mob of farmers on a bunch of green horses," a bitterly resented example of what was regarded as British chauvinism. Within two weeks of the contingent's arrival it rained virtually without stop for a solid month, turning the turf of Salisbury Plain to knee-deep mud. A strong wind with accompanying sleet, hail, and snow blew the tents down. The Plain became a nightmare. Feeling forgotten, the force started to disintegrate. Men went absent without leave to local villages and to London, where low morale and resentment at Canadian rates of pay provoked fighting between the Canadian and British troops. To add to their misery, Sam Hughes insisted that the troops not be allowed alcohol. Moreover, the huts built for the troops were so overcrowded and badly ventilated that there were outbreaks of influenza, bronchitis, and meningitis, which ceased when the rains stopped and proper training began.

Morrison recorded the bitterness the men felt during the months on Salisbury Plain, a time which all regarded as "one of the most miserable and useless periods of hardship."[5] The troops received no official news and only followed the course of the war in the casualty lists in the *Times*, which recorded in two or three daily columns the deaths of officers of the finest regiments of the British army. They knew that behind the stiff upper lips of the generals there was a terrible tragedy taking place which threatened the safety of their empire. The Canadians were exasperated by what Morrison called the fools in the War Office and demanded to be taken across the Channel. Morrison wrote: "The truth is that until the Canadian troops had made a world reputation, there was a tendency to impose on them by influential British officers, who never lost an opportunity of dealing with them and their leaders as though they were green and inferior troops."[6]

One of the early fears of the war was that "bacteria kill more than the bullet in warfare," and efforts were made not to "repeat the enteric catastrophe (of) South Africa." Vaccination was not officially compulsory, but the Canadians got around the absence of regulations. Colonel Nasmith reported how he gave a talk on vaccination against typhoid fever to 700 artillery men of the 1st Brigade in Devizes, standing on a loaded ammunition box next to McCrae and Morrison. The next day the great majority of unvaccinated men volunteered for vaccination, and those few who refused were sent to the base depot and replaced by others.

Officers of the 1st Brigade, Canadian Field Artillery, outside their Mess at Devizes, England, in January 1915, fully accoutred with sword and pistol. John McCrae is dressed as a combatant, not a medical officer. (Public Archives of Canada, C 20188)

Front row: Major McCrae, Major Sharman, Lt. Col. Maclaren, Major Britton, Lt. Col. Morrison, Lt. Col. Dodds, Major Ralston, Capt. Durkee, Capt. Cosgrave, Capt. Alderson, Capt. Benson.

Back row: Lt. Storms, Lt. Gillies, Capt. White, Lt. Bick, Capt. Goodeve, Lt. Thackray, Lt. Boville, Lt. Smith, Lt. Helmer, Lt. Matthews, Lt. Young, Lt. Craig, Lt. Blue, Lt. Whitely, Lt. Kelly, Capt. Stewart.

C.L.C. Allinson recalled two stories from this period.

Soon after we arrived on the Plain a chap in one of our batteries felt ill early one night and, instead of waiting until 'Sick Parade' next morning, he went to Major McCrae's tent to get medicine. McCrae was out but his batman was in the tent fixing it up for the night: feigning McCrae's voice he asked the man what his trouble was; the man described his symptoms and the batman said — 'Run around the tent five times — that'll cure you.' Whilst he was doing so, Major McCrae returned and thought the man had gone mad; as soon as he discovered the true situation he took the man inside, fixed him up with the proper medicaments, then sent him back to his Lines. To his batman, McCrae said — 'You're practicing medicine withoutlicence: back home you would be jailed for that; but out here I order you to run around the tent ten times — and if you trip over a rope or a peg, you'll have to start all over again.'

At Brigade H.Q. we had two wagon-team drivers whom I call 'Smith' and 'Jones' who had brought their own heavy-draft horses with them when they enlisted. They had worked in lumber camps in winters and on road-construction in summers: they were excellent at their work and in caring for their teams; but they were real 'boozers.'

A few days before Christmas they were given Xmas leave and drew all the pay coming to them; they headed for the nearest city where there would be no Military Police, which was Bath, 30 miles westward. Inside 24 hours they were so uproariously drunk, and so grossly disturbing the genteel peace of that Cathedral City and aristocratic health resort, that the local constabulary haled them into the lock-up and notified Headquarters; they were brought back to camp on 23rd December, and put in the Guard tent.

Major McCrae knowing that, in the Guard Tent, those two 'prisoners awaiting trial' would get only a poor, and cold, Xmas dinner — and no beer ration — sent Medical Corporal Waller to the Guard Tent at noon Christmas Day with two small bottles containing a dark brown liquid and labelled *To be taken before meals*': one had Smith's name, the other had Jones' so, instead of beer, Smith and Jones each got a good 'dose' of Army rum for their Xmas treat — thanks to Doctor McCrae.[7]

McCrae visited Sir William Osler at Oxford in December and returned with socks for the men, knitted by a sewing-bee which Lady Osler had organized. The war affected the humanitarian Osler badly; Lady Osler wrote, "It is really extraordinary to hear him.... The attitude W.O. is in seems more unreal than anything else — (he) even says vicious things himself about the Kaiser."[8] Osler threw himself into war work by helping to organize medical services.

The Canadians were struck by the prevailing unconcern about the war. "The common talk was that we had stepped in to keep our treaty with France and to assist poor Belgium, whose neutrality had been violated.... Englishmen did not feel that England's fall was first and last the object of Germany's ambition."[9] The Canadians, in contrast, saw a fight between two empires. They were astonished by the able-bodied men in the streets, the unbusinesslike atmosphere of the War Office, the business-as-usual attitude in London, and the strikes for higher pay in the munition factories and shipyards. During the war the Canadian troops on leave in London were increasingly embittered by the lack of awareness of the tragedies being played out less that 70 miles from London.

On 4 November the contingent was inspected by King George V and by Lord Roberts, who said that "it seemed to him that the people of the Colonies were more appreciative of the greatness of the struggle and more patriotic than those at home."[10] In early February the division moved to France. The men made a three-day sea journey to St Nazaire on the Bay of Biscay, were put into freight cars, and fitted up near the Flanders Front with goatskin coats, leather jerkins, and mitts for the trenches. Then, in a trip by train that took three days and two nights, they travelled the 500 miles to Steenwerk, a railroad station 20 miles west of Ypres and 50 miles east of Boulogne. After marching 20 miles to Armentiere and the 'front,' they were attached to a unit of Royal Field Artillery (RFA) and, to gain some experience, they stayed in a chateau with delightful old British officers. A few days later, on 1 March 1915, the divisional artillery moved slightly south to take over the positions of another RFA brigade and soon they were involved in small artillery fights. The division was part of General Sir Douglas Haig's First Army. Haig suggested that the Canadians pretend to be English, since if the Germans thought they were Canadians they were more likely to be attacked.

The German "Schlieffen" war plan had been to crush France by a rapid attack while holding Russia at bay; in order to accomplish this goal the Germans had to by-pass the French system of forts and attack through Belgium and Northern France, going south to Paris in a gradually wheeling arc. The refusal of Belgium to allow free passage had brought Britain into the war. The German wheeling sweep was far wider than the French had expected and the battle shifted from France to Flanders in Belgium as both sides tried to turn the other's flank. In the end, they failed to outflank each other and so began the "race to the sea." By October 1914 the war of movement was over. Both sides were locked in a system of trenches stretching from the Swiss frontier to the North Sea, defended by barbed wire, machine guns, and artillery. In October and November the small British army was exhausted by poorly directed attacks on the Germans in Flanders — the "First Battle of Ypres." By the end of 1914 there was a deadlock on the western front. On the German side, General Falkenhayn realized that a long war in the west was inevitable and turned his attention to the eastern front, as Churhill turned his attention to the Dardanelles.

From 10-12 March 1915 the Canadian artillery took part in the battle of Neuve Chapelle. At a great price the men accomplished their mission "to straighten out the line," and they won high praise from the indecisive Sir John French for their efforts. The artillery then moved back to Fleurbaix. Morrison recalled visiting the scene of the battlefield with McCrae and being spotted by the Germans, who fired on them for 15 minutes with a low-calibre field gun while they lay in the furrows of a ploughed field. McCrae described his part in the battle of Neuve Chapelle to his friend Dr C.F. Martin of Montreal:

We have been in the firing line for nearly a month, in our first position as well as this one. Our guns are in action every day and some nights, and for the last week things have been very active, for we are less than four miles away from ... (Neuve Chapelle). The artillery fire from our side was terrible: for 2 hours guns fired like the noise of a machine gun. There were nearly a quarter of a million men engaged on both sides, and the Ger. casualties for the first two days was estimated at 18,000. Firing never dies down entirely: yesterday morning I was down observing in the house behind the trenches (in lack of any other field officer to go) and they began to shell it: we had to take to the cellar, and while there they knocked the end off the house: coming back I got a sniper at me, but he made a good miss. We are much troubled by snipers behind our lines, disguised as Tommies or else civilians. They get a good many men too.

Canadian Field Artillery bringing up the guns. Vimy Ridge, April, 1917. Photograph taken during the Battle of Vimy Ridge. (Public Archives of Canada, PA 1073)

Medically, work is light, for the men are very fit. I met General Carleton Jones the other day, and he opened up about my name appearing in the papers as appointed to the McGill Hospital (he took exception to the name). He intimated that my movements depended on him, and I intimated that I didn't greatly care which way it went. This in a sufficiently pleasant way — and sorry too that Charley Peters was put out about it. He had done good and long service."[11]

To his mother he wrote on 30 March:

I attend the gun lines; any casualty is reported by telephone and I go to it. The wounded and sick stay where they are till dark, when the field ambulance go over certain grounds and collect. A good deal of suffering is entailed by the delay till night, but it is useless for vehicles to go on the roads within 1500 yards of the trenches. They are willing enough to go. Most of the trench injuries are of the head, and therefore there is a high proportion of killed in the daily warfare as opposed to an attack. Our Canadian plots fill up rapidly.[12]

Heavy fighting and the restrictive practice of the British skilled trade unions against the use of unskilled labour in the munitions factories meant that there was a great shortage of artillery ammunition. After the battle of Neuve Chapelle the field artillery was limited to 15 rounds per gun per day. The shortage became so acute that the ration was lowered to three rounds per gun per day, and these to be fired only "for essential purposes." Allinson told the story that in late March McCrae visited the observation posts of the batteries near the front-line. At one of them he saw a German battery moving in the open, apparently aware of the British shortage of shells. McCrae ordered the four guns into action and knocked out the German batttery, using up 200 shells in the process — the emergency ration of the whole Canadian artillery for one day. McCrae and Morrison were called to divisional headquarters to explain their "violation of Army orders." Though the story is probably exaggerated, there is no doubt that an incident of this type did occur, not necessarily involving McCrae. Alderson later reported that "knocking out an enemy battery moving in an exposed position in broad daylight" was an essential objective according to South African standards and that military zeal had led to an "error of judgement." McCrae's ambivalent position as both brigade surgeon and second-in-command led to difficulties with the younger officers. It was reported later that "he nearly caused a mutiny by giving artillery orders on the authority of his medical rank, in the absence of his friend the Colonel" and "though a perfectly good artillery man in the Boer War ... did not realize that things had changed between 1901 and 1915."[13]

McCrae lectured to the batteries about the importance of sanitation, particularly in trench warfare, and uttered threats as to what he would do if he found a battery with lice. After dining one evening at the officers' mess of one of the batteries, he could not sleep when he returned to brigade headquarters because he was itching so much. Next day he took lye-soap, useful against lice, and started to wash in the barnyard trough. At that moment the Germans started shelling the farmhouse, and the staff scattered for the fields, with McCrae running naked down the road until, as a shell fell near him, he dived into a muddy ditch. After the shelling stopped he called for a towel and returned to the farmhouse, cursing the lousy battery and later ordering the men to the delousing station at Hazebrouck. There, curiously enough, they too were apparently shelled and raced naked into the street, cheered by the Flemish women of the town.[14]

Interior of Ypres Cathedral. November, 1917. (Public Archives of Canada, PA 2132)

84

CHAPTER ELEVEN
IN FLANDERS FIELDS

On 1 April the men of the Canadian division were pulled out of the firing line and sent into rest billets, and on the 6th they were moved to Oudezele, 10 miles west of Ypres, as part of General Smith-Dorrien's Second Army. They trained in trench warfare and were ordered to relieve a French division north and east of Ypres on 20 and 21 of April. It was a quiet sector of the front with a poor line of trenches; a tacit semi-truce between the French and Germans in that area had left the front-line defences inadequate. There was little intimation of the coming German attack. The Ypres salient, as it was known, bulged into German-held territory; it was eight miles wide and about six miles deep, and was dominated by higher enemy ground on three sides. Everyone entering the salient had to go on the Poperinghe-Ypres road, through the increasingly devastated city of Ypres. During the course of the war the salient was one huge artillery target which resulted in the loss of nearly a half-million Allied troops. It was a perpetual grouse in the army that it should have been abandoned and the casualties prevented.

McCrae wrote at least twice weekly to his mother; just before the second battle of Ypres he received a letter from her which said: "Take good care of my son Jack, but I would not have you unmindful that, sometimes, when we save we lose." He wrote later that "Often when I had to go out over the areas that were being shelled, it (his mother's letter) came into my mind. I would shoulder the (first aid) box, and 'go to it.'

The Canadian infantry held a line in the centre of the Ypres salient bulge about 2¼ miles long. To their right were three British divisions, and to their left, running to the Yser Canal, the French 45th Algerian Division with the French 87th Territorial Division just beyond it. The Canadian infantry moved up on 17 April and the artillery later. The artillery was sent into the Ypres salient in stages. Morrison was critical of the tactics which left the guns dispersed when the attack came. McCrae's brigade was in reserve on 21 April. When the French divisional commander, General Ferry, handed over his section of the line to the Canadians, he warned them of the rumours of an impending attack with poison gas which had been given by German prisoners and deserters who even carried primitive gas masks. For reporting this rumour Ferry was later dismissed by his army. From 20 April a giant Krupp howitzer continuously dropped one-ton shells into Ypres, so that by the 22nd panic-stricken Belgian civilians were rapidly leaving the beautiful city, which was steadily reduced to rubble during the rest of the war.

On the afternoon of 22 April a light breeze was blowing towards the west. In defiance of the Hague conventions of 1899 and 1906, the Germans released chlorine gas along the French front, accompanying it by a fearful artillery barrage. The gas was released on a front of about three miles and reached a height of up to 100 feet, being seen as a yellow-green curtain rolling over the French lines at six miles per hour. The French Moroccan conscripts and territorials died, or broke and ran, leaving a three-mile gap on the left of the bulge. The Germans poured into the gap, turning the flank of the Canadian division and threatening to cut off the entire Ypres salient and to surround the Canadian and British divisions. They attacked with eight divisions of men, but were cautious, partly because of fear of their own gas and partly because failing light prevented them from knowing the extent of their success. They dug in where they were at 7:30 p.m.

McCrae's brigade was ordered up to the line. He wrote:

> As we moved up last evening, there was heavy firing about 4:30 on the left, the hour at which the general attack with gas was made when the French line broke. We could see the shells bursting over Ypres, and in a small village ... (we were) ordered ... to halt.... As we sat on the road we began to see the French stragglers — men with arms, wounded men, teams, wagons, civilians, refugees — some by the roads, some across country, all talking, shouting — the very picture of *debacle*. I must say they were 'tag-enders' of a fighting line, rather than the line itself. They streamed on, and shouted to us scraps of not too inspiriting information while we stood and took our medicine, and picked out gun positions in case we had to go in there and then. The men were splendid; not a word; not a shake, and it was a terrific test. Traffic whizzed by — ambulances, transport, ammunition, supplies, despatch riders — and the shells thundered into the town, or burst high in the air nearer us, and the refugees streamed. Women, old men, little children, hopeless, tearful, quiet or excited, tired or dodging the traffic, — and the wounded in singles or in groups. Here and there I could give a momentary help, and the ambulance picked up as they could. So the cold moonlight night wore on — no change save that the towers of Ypres showed up against the glare of the city burning; and the shells still sailed in.

Morrison described the massive rabble of Moroccan French troops running obliquely towards the Canadians who formed a wedge to cut them off. Some of them dropped off horses, wagons, ambulances, and lay curled up on the ground, struggling, foaming at the mouth, and breathing stertorously. Hundreds of old and decrepit men and women passed them on hay-wagons, which were drawn by small boys, goats, crippled old horses, and any beast of burden available. Two Canadian infantry regiments went up to the line, singing *It's a long way to Tipperary* despite the horrific scenes. The Canadian artillerymen roared in ecstasy at the sight of these men, and "a gassed Turco lying in the road of the column raised himself on his hands, and with glazing eyes, shrieked something in Arabic, reeled out of the way of the column, and fell dead."[2] Of the second battle of Ypres, Morrison wrote that "the stand (the

Canadians) made was one of the most gallant and courageous deeds in the history of war, and the advance of their reserves was a magnificent sight that will never be forgotten by those who witnessed it."[3] Morrison went forward to investigate what was happening and found that it was "gas" — but since it was the first time he had heard of "gas" he was not much the wiser.

McCrae wrote:

At 9:30 our ammunition column ... appeared ... and we prepared to send forward ammunition as soon as we could learn where the batteries had taken up position in retiring, for retire they had to. Eleven, twelve, and finally grey day broke, and we still waited. At 3:45 word came to go in to support a French counterattack at 4:30 a.m. Hastily we got the order spread; it was 4 a.m. and three miles to go.

Of one's feelings all this night — of the asphyxiated French soliders — of the women and children — of the cheery steady British reinforcements that moved up quietly past us, going up, not back — I could write, but you can imagine.

We took the road at once, and went up at the gallop. The Colonel (Morrison) rode ahead to scout a position (we had only four guns, part of the ammunition column, and the brigade staff; the 1st and 4th batteries were back in reserve at our last billet). Along the roads we went, and made our place on time, pulled up for ten minutes just short of the position, where I put Bonfire with my groom in a farmyard, and went forward on foot — only a quarter of a mile or so — then we advanced.

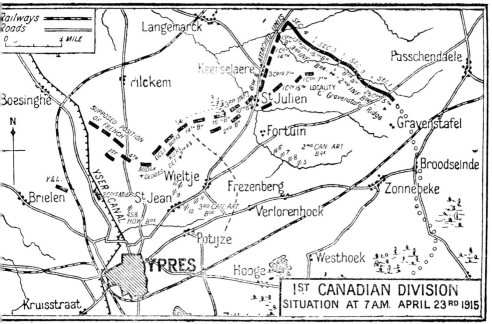

With permission of Geographia Ltd.

Bonfire had soon to move; a shell killed a horse about four yards away from him, and he wisely took other ground. Meantime we went into the position on the Yser canal we were to occupy for seventeen days, though we could not guess that.

We got into action at once, under heavy gunfire. We were to the left entirely of the British line, and behind French troops, and so we remained for eight days. A Colonel of the R.A., known to fame, joined us and camped with us; he was our link with the French Headquarters, and was in local command of the guns in this locality. When he left us eight days later he said, 'I am glad to get out of this hell-hole.' He was a great comfort to us, for he is very capable, and the entire battle was largely fought 'on our own,' following the requests of the Infantry on our front, and scarcely guided by our own staff at all. We at once set out to register our targets, and almost at once had to get into steady firing on quite a large sector of front. We dug in the guns as quickly as we could, and took as Headquarters some infantry trenches already sunk on a ridge near the canal. We were subject from the first to a steady and accurate shelling, for we were all in sight, as were the German trenches about 2000 yards to our front. At times the fire would come in salvoes quickly repeated. Bursts of fire would be made for ten of fifteen minutes at a time. We got all varieties of projectile, from 3 inch to 8 inch, or perhaps 10 inch; the small ones usually as air bursts, the larger percussions in air, and the heaviest percussion only.

My work began almost from the start — steady but never overwhelming, except perhaps once for a few minutes. A little cottage behind our ridge served as a cook-house, but was so heavily hit the second day that we had to be chary of it. During bursts of fire I usually took the back slope of the sharply crested ridge for what shelter it offered. At 3 our 1st and 4th arrived, and went into action at once a few hundred yards in our rear. Wires were at once put out, to be cut by shells hundreds and hundreds of times, but always repaired by our indefatigable linemen. So the day wore on; in the night the shelling still kept up: three different German attacks were made and repulsed. If we suffered by being close up, the Germans suffered from us, for already tales of good shooting came down to us. I got some sleep despite the constant firing, for we had none last night.

On the night of 22 April, some Canadians made a brave counterattack, retaking Kitchener's Wood for a short time but losing half their 1,500 men. There was no major German activity on the 23rd, and by evening some sort of defence line had been made by 21 depleted British and Canadian battalions, which faced 42 German battalions and a German artillery of 5:1 superiority. Several gallant but futile British counterattacks failed during the day.

At 4 a.m. on 24 April three red flares went up from a German observation balloon at Westroosebeke, and shellfire pounded the Canadian trenches. Then a line of ghostly figures rose from the German trenches and released chlorine from hoses, the green-yellow cloud drifting onto the 8th and 15th Canadian battalions, suffocating many of them. Waves of German infantry poured into the Canadian lines, eventually forcing the Canadians back. The Canadians were hamstrung by their Ross rifles, another of Sam Hughes' legacies, which jammed during rapid firing. Losses among the Canadian battalions were fearful. Good artillery shooting prevented the Germans from exploiting the breach. In the afternoon they took St Julien but were forced back later.

McCrae wrote of 24 April:

Behold us now anything less than two miles north of Ypres on the west side of the canal; this runs north, each bank flanked with high elms, with bare trunks of the familiar Netherlands type. A few yards to the west a main road runs, likewise bordered; ... on the high bank between these we had our headquarters; the ridge is perhaps fifteen to twenty feet high, and slopes forward fifty yards to the water, the back is more steep, and slopes quickly to a little subsidiary water way, deep but dirty. Where the guns were I shall not say; but they were not far, and the German aeroplanes that viewed us daily with all but impunity knew very well. A road crossed over the canal, and interrupted the ridge; across the road from us was our billet — the place we cooked in, at least, and where we usually took our meals. Looking to the south between the trees, we could see the ruins of the city: to the front on the sky line, with rolling ground in front, pitted by French trenches, the German lines; to the left front, several farms and a windmill and farther left, again near the canal, thicker trees and more farms. The farms and windmills were soon burnt. Several farms we used for observing posts were also quickly burnt during the next three or four days. All along behind us at varying distances French and British guns; the flashes at night lit up the sky.

These high trees were at once a protection and a danger. Shells that struck them were usually destructive. When we came in the foliage was still very thin. Along the road, which was constantly shelled 'on spec' by the Germans, one saw all the sights of war: wounded men limping or carried, ambulances, trains of supply, troops, army mules, and tragedies. I saw one bicycle orderly: a shell exploded and he seemed to pedal on for eight or ten revolutions and then collapsed in a heap — dead. Straggling soldiers would be killed or wounded, horses also, until it got to be a nightmare. I used to shudder every time I saw wagons or troops on that road. My dugout looked out on it. I got a square hole, 8 by 8, dug in the side of the hill (west), roofed over with the remnants to keep out the rain, and a little sandbag parapet on the back to prevent pieces of 'back-kick shells' from coming in, or prematures from our own or the French guns for that matter. Some straw on the floor completed it. The ground was treacherous and a slip the first night nearly buried ... so we had to be content with walls straight up and down, and trust to the height of the bank for safety. All places along the bank were more or less alike, all squirrel holes.

This morning we supported a heavy French attack at 4:30; there had been three German attacks in the night, and everyone was tired. We got heavily shelled. In all eight or ten of our trees were cut by shells — cut right off, the upper part of the tree subsiding heavily and straight down, as a usual thing. One would think a piece a foot wide was instantly cut out; and these trees were about 18 inches in diameter. The gas fumes came very heavily: some blew down from the infantry trenches, some came from the shells: one's eyes smarted, and breathing was very laboured. Up to noon to-day we fired 2500 rounds. Last night Col. Morrison and I slept at a French Colonel's headquarters nearby, and in the night our room was filled up with wounded. I woke up and shared my bed with a chap with 'a wounded leg and a chill.' Propably thirty wounded were brought into the one little room.

Col. ..., R.A., kept us in communication with the French General in whose command we were. I bunked down in the trench on the top of the ridge: the sky was red with the glare of the city still burning, and we could hear the almost constant procession of large shells sailing over from our left front into the city: the crashes of their explosion shook the ground where we were. After a terribly hard day, professionally and otherwise, I slept well, but it rained and the trench was awfully muddy and wet.

On 25 April a fresh regular brigade of five British battalions was thrown into the attack near St Julien — and were mown down by German machine guns; 2,400 men were lost in a few minutes. McCrae wrote of this day:

The weather brightened up and we got at it again. This day we had several heavy attacks, prefaced by heavy artillery fire; these bursts of fire would result in our getting 100 to 150 rounds right on us or nearby: the heavier our fire (which was on the trenches entirely) the heavier theirs.

Our food supply came up at dusk in wagons, and the water was any we could get, but of course treated with chloride of lime. The ammunition had to be brought down the roads at the gallop, and the more firing the more wagons. The men would quickly carry the rounds to the guns, as the wagons had to halt behind our hill. The good old horses would swing around at the gallop, pull up in an instant, and stand puffing and blowing, but with their heads up, as if to say, 'Wasn't that well done?' It makes you want to kiss their dear old noses, and assure them of a peaceful pasture once more. To-day we got our dressing station dugout complete, and slept there at night.

Three farms in succession burned on our front — colour in the otherwise dark. The flashes of shells over the front and rear in all directions. The city still burning and the procession still going on. I dressed a number of French wounded; one Turco prayed to Allah and Mohammed all the time I was dressing his wound. On the front field one can see the dead lying here and there, and in places where an assault has been there they lie very thick on the front slopes of the German trenches. Our telephone wagon team was hit by a shell; two horses killed and another wounded. I did what I could for the wounded one, and he subsequently got well. This night, beginning after dark, we got a terrible shelling, which kept up till 2 or 3 in the morning. Finally I got to sleep, though it was still going on. We must have got a couple of hundred rounds, in single or pairs. Every one burst over us, would light up the dugout, and every hit in front would shake the ground and bring down small bits of earth on us, or else the earth thrown into the air by the explosion would come splattering down on our roof, and into the front of the dugout. Col. Morrison tried the mess house, but the shelling was too heavy, and he and the adjutant joined Cosgrave and me, and we four spent an anxious night there in the dark. One officer was on watch 'on the bridge' (as we called the trench at the top of the ridge) with the telephones.

To Billy Turner he wrote:

For 36 hours we had not an infantryman between us and the Germans and this gap was 1200 to 1500 yards wide. God knows why the G. did not put in a big force to eat us up. We really expected to die.[4]

To C.F. Martin he wrote:

Throughout 3 nights they shelled us continuously: and the firing never ceased one consecutive minute night or day: and yet the birds kept singing in the trees — what trees were not cut down by shells.[5]

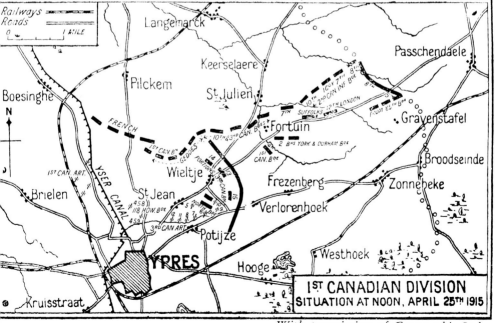

With permission of Geographia Ltd.

The remains of the Canadian's front-line infantry were withdrawn in the evening and night of the 25th. They had lost over 6,000 of their 10,000 men and their efforts were recognized around the empire, Field Marshall Sir John French stating to King George V that "the Canadians Saved the Day." By the night of the 25th a German breakthrough was no longer possible, in part because of the mettle of the Canadians. The Canadian artillery remained in action.

At this stage General Smith-Dorrien proposed abandoning the salient, a suggestion for which he was forced to resign his command by Field Marshall French. For the next month the British attacked; according to official history:

> The governing idea was that the French should restore the line lost by them, and the British should assist.... General Foch ordered immediate counterattacks, which General Putz was not in a position to execute: whilst the British wholehearted attempts to carry out their share by means of offensive action, which was as a rule neither a true counterattack, nor a deliberately prepared attack, led to heavy losses without restoring the situation.... It seemed to the British officers at the front that they were being sacrificed to gain time until the French were ready for a spectacular effort ... this ... did not materialize.[6]

McCrae's brigade headquarters was sited at the point where a west-to-east road from Poperinghe intersected the north-to-south road running along the canal towards Ypres. The four batteries were concentrated 400 yards to the rear. A shell hole on the top of the canal bank was the brigade fire control post, and telephone lines ran to all batteries, to some farm houses along the canal used as forward observation posts, and to the ammunition column 1½ miles back. A partly wrecked farmhouse was the billet for the officers. There were no British troops in front of the brigade, and the wounded were mostly Frenchmen or Algerians. Some of the *poilus*, wounded on top of the canal bank, actually rolled down the bank to the first aid post, McCrae commenting that "the hospitals at Montreal did not have a delivery service like this."[7] Nearby was a small burying ground in which were graves of Belgians and British from "First Ypres," and of French and brigade casualties from the current battle. McCrae's post looked out onto the west-to-east road where reinforcements and supplies came up and casualties returned. After the battle he wrote to Dr Billy Turner:

> During the battle of April 22 to April 25 when the infantry fight was at its acute stage General Turner told us he never saw General Alderson and during the 17 days we never saw Burstall and only 3 times any of his staff. Enough said! Morrison's work was magnificent and he, of all the Brigadiers Infantry and Artillery, was left out of despatches. Jack Coulman was so unfortunate as to have to go into hospital the 2nd or 3rd day, his adjutant likewise, and he (Jack) got mention. (Between friends, my own name went up and got cut out.) There were only 3 mentions for

the 1st Bde. and one of them was a corporal who got killed. Burstall's excuse to Morrison was that 'he had been very busy.'[8]

It was a standard indictment by the troops that the staff were too scared to visit the front line. C.L.C. Allinson wrote that McCrae's orders were to stay in his first aid post but that he often broke them to tend for the wounded outside. Allinson was impressed by McCrae's courage and felt that he should have been awarded a medal for gallantry.

The next days were described by McCrae in letters to his mother:

Monday, 26 April, 1915
Another day of heavy actions, but last night much French and British artillery has come in, and the place is thick with Germans. There are many prematures (with so much firing) but the pieces usually spread before they get to us. It is disquieting, however, I must say. And all the time the birds sing in the trees over our heads. Yesterday up to noon we fired 3000 rounds for the twenty-four hours; to-day we have fired much less, but we have registered fresh fronts, and burned some farms behind the German trenches. About six the fire died down, and we had a peaceful evening and night, and Cosgrave and I in the dugout made good use of it. The Colonel has an individual dugout, and Dodds sleeps 'topside' in the trench. To all this, put a background of anxiety lest the line break, for we are just where it broke before.

Tuesday, 27 April, 1915
This morning again registering batteries on new points. At 1:30 a heavy attack was prepared by the French and ourselves. The fire was very heavy for half an hour and the enemy got busy too. I had to cross over to the batteries during it, an unpleasant journey. More gas attacks in the afternoon. The French did not appear to press the attack hard, but in the light of subsequent events it probably was only a feint. It seems likely that about this time our people began to thin out the artillery again for use elsewhere; but this did not at once become apparent. At night usually the heavies farther back take up the story, and there is a duel. The Germans fire on our roads after dark to catch reliefs and transport. I suppose ours do that same.

Wednesday, 28 April, 1915
I have to confess to an excellent sleep last night. At times anxiety says, 'I don't want a meal,' but experience says 'you need your food,' so I attend regularly to that. The billet is not too safe either. Much German air reconnaissance is over us, and heavy firing from both sides during the day, but the infantry made little attempt to go on. We are perhaps the 'chopping block,' and our 'preparations' may be chiefly designed to prevent detachments of troops being sent from out front elsewhere.

I have said nothing of what goes on on our right and left; but it is equally part and parcel of the whole game; this eight mile front is constantly heavily engaged. At intervals, too, they bombard Ypres. Our back lines, too, have to be constantly shifted on account of shell fire, and we have desultory but constant losses there. In the evening rifle fire gets more frequent, and bullets are constantly singing over us. Some of them are probably ricochets, for we are 1800 yards, or nearly, from the nearest German trench.

Thursday, 29 April, 1915

This morning our billet was hit. We fire less these days, but still a good deal. There was a heavy French attack on our left. The 'gas' attacks can be seen from here. The yellow cloud rising up is for us a signal to open, and we do. The wind is from our side to-day, and a good thing it is. Several days ago during the firing a big Oxford-grey dog, with beautiful brown eyes, came to us in a panic. He ran to me, and pressed his head *hard* against my leg. So I got him to a safe place and he sticks by us. We call him Fleabag, for he looks like it.

This night they shelled us again heavily for some hours — the same shorts, hits, overs on percussion, and great yellow-green air bursts. One feels awfully irritated by the constant din — a mixture of anger and apprehension.

Friday, 30 April, 1915

Thick mist this morning, and relative quietness; but before it cleared the Germans started again to shell us. At 10 it cleared, and from 10 to 2 we fired constantly. The French advanced, and took some ground on our left front and a batch of prisoners. This was at the place we call Twin Farms. Our men looked curiously at the Boches as they were marched through. Some better activity in the afternoon by the Allies' aeroplanes. The German planes have had it too much their way lately. Many of to-day's shells have been very large — 10 or 12 inch; a lot of tremendous holes dug in the fields just behind us.

Saturday, 1 May, 1915

May day! Heavy bombardment at intervals through the day. Another heavy artillery preparation at 3:25, but no French advance. We fail to understand why, but orders go. We suffered somewhat during the day. Through the evening and night heavy firing at intervals.

Sunday, 2 May, 1915

Heavy gunfire again this morning. Lieut. H(elmer) was killed at the guns. His diary's last words were, 'It has quieted a little and I shall try to get a good sleep.' I said the Commital Service over him, as well as I could from memory. A soldier's death! Batteries again registering barrages or barriers of fire at set ranges. At 3 the Germans attacked, preceded by gas clouds. Fighting went on for an hour and a half, during which their guns hammered heavily with some loss to us. The French lines are very uneasy, and we are correspondingly anxious. The infantry fire was heavy, and we fired incessantly, keeping on into the night. Despite the heavy fire I got asleep at 12, and slept until daylight which comes at 3.

Lieutenant Alex Helmer was killed by a direct hit of an 8-inch shell while he was going to the 2nd Battery. A couple of men went to the burying ground when the shelling stopped and dug his grave; others picked up as many pieces of the body as they could, putting them into sandbags which were laid in an army blanket in the form of a body, the blanket being fastened by big safety pins. After sun-down a small group of men who could be spared buried him. McCrae and Captain Cosgrave were at the burial of their close friend. No lights could be exposed and McCrae, deeply affected, recited from memory some passages from the Church of England's "Order of Burial of the Dead."[9]

A raw wooden cross, marked "Alexis Helmer, Lieut. 2nd Bty, C.F.A. 2nd May 1915," was planted in the soil over the grave.

It was Helmer's death which, according to some accounts, inspired McCrae to write the poem *In Flanders Fields*.

> In Flanders fields the poppies blow
> Between the crosses, row on row,
> That mark our place; and in the sky
> The larks, still bravely singing, fly
> Scarce heard amidst the guns below.
>
> We are the Dead. Short days ago
> We lived, felt dawn, saw sunset glow,
> Loved, and were loved, and now we lie
>   In Flanders fields.
>
> Take up our quarrel with the foe:
> To you from failing hands we throw
> The torch; be yours to hold it high.
> If ye break faith with us who die
> We shall not sleep, though poppies grow
>   In Flanders fields.

There are contradictory stories about the writing of this poem, because of the circumstances under which it was written. According to C.L.C. Allinson, McCrae went on fire control duty with Cosgrave after Helmer's funeral, being relieved at 7:30 in the morning. Allinson said that he saw McCrae writing the poem the next day while sitting on the rearstep of an ambulance and looking at Helmer's grave; after McCrae read the poem to him he, Allinson, memorized it and later wrote it down.[10] Cosgrave said, however, that Helmer was buried at 11 a.m. on the 2nd, and that McCrae, grief-stricken, left the dugout and, in an attempt to compose his mind, wrote the poem in 20 minutes.[11] Morrison recorded that McCrae said he wrote the poem to pass away the time between the arrivals of batches of wounded.[12] This seems most likely. At some stage, according to yet another account, McCrae apparently crumpled up the paper on which the poem was written, but the discarded poem was rescued and read by Captain F.A.C. Scrimger, who persuaded him to have it published. Other stories say that it was Morrison who persuaded him not to discard it but to send it for publication.

Whatever the truth, McCrae eventually sent the poem to the *Spectator* but it was returned (McCrae saying — "The babe hath returned to its mother's arms").[13] It was then sent to *Punch*, apparently with some other poems. *In Flanders Fields* was published in *Punch* on 8 Dec. 1915.

The second battle of Ypres continued.

Monday, 3 May, 1915
A clear morning, and the accursed German aeroplanes over our positions again. They are usually fired at, but no luck. To-day a shell on our hill dug out a cannon ball about six inches in diameter — probably of Napoleon's or earlier times — heavily rusted. A German attack began, but half an hour of artillery fire drove it back. Major ..., R.A. was up forward, and could see the German reserves. Our 4th was turned on: first round 100 over; shortened and went into gunfire, and his report that the effect was perfect. The same occurred again in the evening, and again at midnight. The Germans were reported to be constantly massing for attack, and we as constantly "went to them." The Germans shelled us as usual at intervals. This must get very tiresome to read; but through it all, it must be mentioned that the constantly broken communications have to be mended, rations and ammunition brought up, the wounded to be dressed and got away. Our dugouts have the French Engineers and French Infantry next door by turns. They march in and out. The back of the hill is a network of wires, so that one has to go carefully.

Tuesday, 4 May, 1915
Despite intermittent shelling and some casualties the quietest day yet; but we live in an uneasy atmosphere as German attacks are constantly being projected, and our communications are interrupted and scrappy. We get no news of any sort and have just to sit tight and hold on. Evening closed in rainy and dark. Our dugout is very slenderly provided against it, and we get pretty wet and very dirty. In the quieter morning hours we get a chance of a wash and occasionally a shave.

Wednesday, 5 May, 1915
Heavily hammered in the morning from 7 to 9, but at 9 it let up; the sun came out and things looked better. Evidently our line has again been thinned of artillery and the requisite minimum to hold is left. There were German attacks to our right, just out of our area. Later on we and they both fired heavily, the first battery getting it especially hot. The planes

over us again and again, to coach the guns. An attack expected at dusk, but it turned only to heavy night shelling, so that with our fire, theirs and the infantry cracking away constantly, we got sleep in small quantity all night; bullets whizzing over us constantly. Heavy rain from 5 to 8, and everything wet except the far-in corner of the dugout, where we mass our things to keep them as dry as we may.

Thursday, 6 May, 1915

After the rain a bright morning; the leaves and blossoms are coming out. We ascribe our quietude to a welcome flock of allied planes which are over this morning. The Germans attacked at eleven, and again at six in the afternoon, each meaning a waking up of heavy artillery on the whole front. In the evening we had a little rain at intervals, but it was light.

Friday, 7 May, 1915

A bright morning early, but clouded over later. The Germans gave it to us very heavily. There was heavy fighting to the south-east of us. Two attacks or threats and we went in again.

Saturday, 8 May, 1915

For the last three days we have been under British divisional control, supporting our own men who have been put farther to the left, till they are almost in front of us. It is an added comfort. We have four officers out with various infantry regiments for observation and cooperation; they have to stick it in trenches, as all the houses and barns are burned. The whole front is constantly ablaze with gunfire; the racket never ceases. We have now to do most of the work for our left, as our line appears to be much thinner than it was. A German attack followed the shelling at 7; we were fighting hard till 12, and less regularly all the afternoon. We suffered much, and at one time were down to seven guns. Of these two were smoking at every joint, and the levers were so hot that the gunners used sacking for their hands. The pace is now much hotter, and the needs of the infantry for fire more insistent. The guns are in bad shape by reason of dirt, injuries and heat. The wind fortunately blows from us, so there is no gas, but the attacks are still very heavy. Evening brought a little quiet, but very disquieting news (which afterwards proved untrue); and we had to face a possible retirement. You may imagine our state of mind, unable to get anything sure in the uncertainty, except that we should stick out as long as the guns would fire and we could fire them. That sort of night brings a man down to his 'bare skin,' I promise you. The night was very cold, and not a cheerful one.

Sunday, 9 May, 1915

At 4 we were ordered to get ready to move, and the Adjutant picked out new retirement positions; but a little better news came, and the daylight and sun revived us a bit. As I sat in my dugout a little white and black dog with tan spots bolted in over the parapet, during heavy firing, and going to the farthest corner began to dig furiously. Having scraped out a pathetic little hole two inches deep, she sat down and shook, looking most plaintively at me. A few minutes, her owner came along, a French soldier. Bissac was her name, but she would not leave me at the time. When I sat down a little later, she stole out and shyly crawled between me and the wall; she stayed by me all day, and I hope got later to safe quarters.

Firing kept up all day. In thirty hours we had fired 3600 rounds, and at times with seven, eight, or nine guns; our wire cut and repaired eighteen times. Orders came to move, and we got ready. At dusk we got the guns out by hand, and all batteries assembled at a given spot in comparative safety. We were much afraid they would open up on us, for at 10 o'clock they gave us 100 or 150 rounds, hitting the trench parapet again and again. However, we were up the road, the last wagon half a mile away before they opened. One burst near me, and splattered some pieces around, but we got clear, and by 12 were out of the usual fire zone. Marched all night, tired as could be, but happy to be clear.

I was glad to get on dear old Bonfire again. We made about sixteen miles, and got to our billets at dawn. I had three or four hours' sleep, and arose to a peaceful breakfast. We shall go back to the line elsewhere very soon, but it is a present relief, and the next place is sure to be better, for it cannot be much worse. Much of this narrative is bald and plain, but it tells our part in a really great battle. I have only had hasty notes to go by; in conversation there is much one could say that would be of greater interest. Heard of the Lusitania disaster on our road out. A terrible affair![14]

After the Canadian artillery was withdrawn, McCrae set forth his reflections on the battle to his mother:

Northern France, 10 May, 1915
We got here to refit and rest this monring at 4, having marched last night at 10. The general impression in my mind is of a nightmare. We have been in the most bitter of fights. For seventeen days and seventeen nights none of us have had our clothes off, nor our boots even, except occasionally. In all that time while I was awake, gunfire and rifle fire never ceased for sixty seconds, and it was sticking to our utmost by a weak line all but ready to break, knowing nothing of what was going on, and depressed by reports of anxious infantry. The men and the divisions are worthy of all the praise that can be given. It did not end in four days when many of our infantry were taken out. It kept on at fever heat till yesterday.

This, of course is the second battle of Ypres, or the Battle of the Yser, I do not know which. At one time we were down to seven guns, but those guns were smoking at every joint, the gunners using cloth to handle the breech levers because of the heat. We had three batteries in action with four guns added from the other units. Our casualties were half the number of men in the firing line. The horse lines and the wagon lines farther back suffered less, but the Brigade list has gone far higher than any artillery normal. I know one brigade R.A. that was in the Mons retreat and had about the same. I have done what fell to hand. My clothes, boots, kit, and dugout at various times were sadly bloody. Two of our batteries are reduced to two officers each. We have had constant accurate shellfire, but we have given back no less. And behind it all was the constant background of the sights of the dead, the wounded, the maimed, and a terrible anxiety lest the line should give way.

During all this time, we have been behind French troops, and only helping our own people by oblique fire when necessary. Our horses have suffered heavily too. Bonfire had a light wound from a piece of shell; it is healing and the dear fellow is very fit. Had my first ride for seventeen days last night. We never saw horses but with the wagons bringing up the ammunition. When fire was hottest they had to come two miles on a road terribly swept, and they did it magnificently. But how tired we are! Weary in body and wearier in mind. None of our men went off their heads but men in nearby units did — and no wonder.

By 14 May the brigade had been given new guns and reinforcements and was back in action 50 miles south, at the battle of Festubert. In that battle the British and French attacked well-prepared German defences, often in broad daylight with inadequate artillery, and were decimated by machine gun fire. Failure to take objectives resulted in General Alderson at Canadian Divisional Headquarters being accused by Haig of lack of 'pluck' and 'determination.' The enormous Allied losses convinced the Germans of the strength of their own western defences and the absence of any real threat from the Allies.

In June McCrae was ordered to leave the artillery to join the Canadian Army Medical Corps, and he did so reluctantly. The unexpected, unprecedented massive Allied casualties meant that there was an urgent need for doctors. He wrote that Morrison, Dodds, Cosgrave, and he were very sorry to part; the comradeship they had was deeply felt. He left on 2 June, saying goodbye to Allinson, who reported that McCrae "most un-militarily told (me) what he thought of being transferred to the medicals and being pulled away from his beloved guns. His last words to me were: 'Allinson, all the goddam doctors in the world will not win this bloody war: what we need is more and more fighting men."[15]

McCrae returned to England to join the McGill-raised Number 3 Canadian General Hospital. First, however, he visited the Oslers in Oxford. Lady Osler described how on

Sunday afternoon Jack McCrae came — I am *glad* and *sorry* you did not hear him. He looked thin and worn, but was intensely interesting; 31 days in the trenches with 8 days rest ... he came from (Festubert) last Thursday. His clothes were awful. I have sent everything to the cleaners.

He says the British hatred for the Germans increases daily since the *Lusitania*, and that *he* would not touch the hand of any of the men he knew so well in London two years ago (at the Medical Congress). He feels that the Allies will win but nothing can be ended except by absolute exhaustion. The nerve strain he says is beyond any sensation possible to describe ... they were at it night and day, saving the situation as we know. Really I felt sick when he left Monday night.... Jack lay in the garden all (Monday). We repacked him and sent him off to town (London) at 9:30....[16]

The Hospital at Dannes-Camiers; the Durbar tents were given to the War Office by the Beghum of Scopal, and sent from India. (From "Number 3 Canadian General Hospital (McGill), 1914-1919" by R.C. Fetherstonhaugh. Montreal: Gazette Publishing Company.)

CHAPTER TWELVE
NUMBER 3 CANADIAN GENERAL HOSPITAL: DANNES-CAMIERS, 1915-16

On 1 June 1915 McCrae was posted as lieutenant-colonel in charge of medicine at the Number 3 Canadian General Hospital. With great enthusiasm McGill University had volunteered to equip and operate a 520-bed hospital for service in the war. Sam Hughes accepted the offer but did not pass it on to the War Office in London. Sir William Osler went to London and relayed McGill's proposal to Sir Alfred Keogh, Director of Medical Services, who accepted a 1,040 bed hospital and suggested establishing it in the spring of 1915. There were large numbers of applicants from McGill, including medical students. McCrae, as indicated, was placed in charge of medicine; Lt. Col. J.M. Elder was in charge of surgery. The head was H.S. Birkett. Others on the staff were Edward Archibald, A.C.P. Howard, J.C. Meakins, and W.P.P. Hill as senior officers, and there were 23 junior officers including W.W. Francis, L.J. Rhea, W.E. Turner, and other friends of McCrae. The assistant quarter master was Revere Osler, Sir William's only son. J.G. Adami was a consultant.

The unit, with McCrae, left for France on 17 June and landed at Boulogne on the 18th; it went by train the few miles to Dannes-Camiers, the authorities there having been told of their arrival thirty minutes before the train pulled into the station. There were five other hospitals in the area, including Number 1 Canadian General Hospital (Toronto) and the Harvard Unit. The McGill hospital was under canvas, in Durbar tents given to the War Office by the Begum of Scopal and sent from India.

The hospital accepted its first patients on 8 August. On 20 July it was visited by Sir Robert Borden and on 5 August by Sam Hughes, Max Aitken, and others. Archibald described Hughes as

> rustic, a bit uncouth, but I believe him to be able in practical ways. McCrae thinks him better than the scholarly, educated, obstinate, courteous English officer, the barnacle of the War Office.... McCrae and (C.B.) Keenan are both bitter about the pig-headedness and mistakes of our War Office and of the General Staff; and both testify to the wonderful work of the Line Regiments.[1]

Archibald, McCrae, and Donald Hingston visited Paris for a few days in July. They went to hospitals in the mornings and in the afternoons wandered around, but found Paris empty and dull. A nurse who knew McCrae from Montreal saw him in Paris but did not recognize him since he seemed to have aged 15 years. Also in July, McCrae, Birkett, and Yates visited the front near Plessines and 'Plugstreet' Wood, but did not go into the front line trench because of the risk. At the mess table Archibald recorded a conversation in which McCrae said that "this (war) was the biggest thing since the birth of Christ. Some one else said the Crusades, which Jack would not allow."[2] For McCrae the war was an apocalyptic event.

The role of the hospital was to act as a clearing house for the sick and wounded. Patients were kept for three weeks provided that they were then fit to go to convalescent camp for two to three weeks, and afterwards to be returned to duty. If the heads of surgery and medicine decided that a man could not be returned to active duty in six weeks, he was sent to hospital in England. Those who were too ill to move remained at the hospital, including many with chest wounds and chest wound infections who were in the charge of the physicians. Others were kept at the hospital only for diagnosis, prognosis, and shipped to England, a matter of a few days. Necessary surgery was performed at the hospital, but those requiring elective surgery went to England.

The work of the hospitals was continuous; even on the quietest day along the western front, 7,000 British soldiers were killed or wounded, and the 'wastage' went back to the enormous base hospitals. In the first month of the hospital's operation, small convoys of wounded, mainly from the Ypres Salient, were admitted, including some burnt by flame-throwers. Sir William Osler visited the front from 7-15 September as a lieutenant-colonel in the Royal Army Medical Corps, and was welcomed at the hospital. Many of the staff had been his pupils and all were his friends. He was shown around the medical wards by McCrae and Howard and "all interesting and obscure cases were shown to him as in the old days in Baltimore and we received his simple, concise and invaluable advice, and the patient, the cheery smile and word of encouragement."[3] McCrae and Rhea took him to a dressing station, where the wounded were brought from the trenches, and then to Armentieres and Nieppe but were unable to reach Bailleul or Hazebrouck because of shelling. Osler saw everywhere the machinery of war and the great squares of the graveyards.

The visit was saddened for Osler by the decision of his son Revere, who felt too safe, to join the Imperial Royal Artillery. This decision nearly broke the old man's heart since the life expectancy of a young, combatant officer on the western front was a few months. To what extent McCrae influenced Revere Osler's decision is not known, but Osler wrote in March 1916: "This horrid war may last another 2 years. Revere got home on the 6th to arrange to his transfer to the Imperial Army. He feels he should be in the fighting line, and hopes to join the artillery. He is in A.1. form, hard as nails, and long association with Jack McCrae has made him a bit blood thirsty."[4]

Osler hated the war, hated "the needless slaughter of the brave young fellows — allies and foes alike," the "gross exaggeration of the atrocity stories," the increasing loss of the sons of his friends and of ex-Oxford undergraduates, and the appalling injuries.[5] In October 1915 he gave a talk on science and war in Leeds. He said, bravely in the circumstances:

The pride, pomp, and circumstances of war have so captivated the human mind that its horrors are deliberately minimized.... The inspiration of a nation is its battles.... The French Revolution and the founding of the American Republic seemed to lift humanity to a level on which might be practically realized the brotherhood of man.... An intellectual community had sprung up between nations, fostered by a growing interchange of literature and maintained by gatherings.... And some of us had indulged the fond hope that in the power man had gained over nature had arisen possibilities for intellectual and social development such as to control collectively his morals and emotions, so that the nation would not learn war any more. We were foolish enough to think that where Christianity had failed science might succeed, forgetting that the hopelessness of the failure of the Gospel lay not in its message, but in its interpretation. The promised peace was for the individual.

And yet, Osler could not get away from the Darwinist ideas of the Imperialists. "In spite of unspeakable horrors," he wrote, "war has been one of the master forces in the evolution of a race of beings that has taken several millions of years to reach its present position." Science, which he knew had been used to achieve the incredible progress of the Victorian age, had a darker side when harnessed for destruction. Yet, that having been said, "the wounded soldier would throw his sword into the scale for science — and he is right."[6]

In September 1915 the McGill unit was also visited by Sir Almroth Wright, the famous English bacteriologist who had a research laboratory at Wimereux near Boulogne devoted to investigating the proper treatment of infected wounds. The fearful infection rate among the wounded soldiers was carrying surgeons back to the pre-Listerian days and their generation had no experience in dealing with such infected wounds. One of Wright's assistants was Alexander Fleming, who later wrote: "Surrounded by all those infected wounds, by men who were suffering and dying without our being able to do anything to help them, I was consumed by a desire to discover, after all this struggling and waiting, something which would kill these microbes...."[7]

The majority of patients at the hospital were wounded, and the main concern was the fearful injuries inflicted by artillery fire, which was responsible for three-quarters of all wounds suffered on both sides. These wounds were generally heavily infected, unlike bullet wounds, and treatment was by surgery, by promotion of drainage, and by flushing with Almroth Wright's saline solution. On the medical side there were some conditions peculiar to the war. These included trench foot, caused by standing in the semi-liquid mud or water at the bottom of the trenches; bronchitis, practically universal in front-line troops; trench fever, caused by lice infestation; war nephritis; soldiers' heart, caused by continuous or excessive cigarette smoking; gas poisoning; and war or shell shock, a severe nervous collapse associated with extreme anxiety. Mild symptoms of nervous disorder such as stammering or difficulty in talking were common among all the patients.

In late September the hospital was ordered to evacuate all movable patients

Officers of Number 3 Canadian General Hospital (McGill), Dannes-Camiers. From left: A.T. Henderson, W.G. Turner, H.M. Little, R.H. Malone, F.W. Tidmarsh, J.A. MacMillan, H.C. Dixon, R.B. Robinson, H.C. Burgess, W.T. Ewing, H.S. Birkett, L.H. McKim, J.M. Elder, Lt. Col. Shillington, J.G. Browne, H.B. Yates, J.C. Wickham, E.W. Archibald, A.H. Pirie, John McCrae, W.W. Francis. (McCrae Birthplace Museum)

in preparation for the casualties expected from the battle of Loos, a joint British-French attack which marked the first appearance in strength of Kitchener's New Armies. The attack against heavily defended positions, with an inadequate artillery support which served mainly to lose the element of surprise, was a costly failure with 250,000 Allied and 140,000 German casualties. During the week of the battle 1,000 casualties, many with fearful shell wounds, were admitted to Dannes-Camiers.

On 25 October severe storms led to flooding of the wards, tearing of the canvas, and pulling up of the tents. The first blood transfusion was carried out in October, with spectacular results. In November the weather became worse — the effects of frosts and icy winds and rain on the tented hospital were so serious that the hospital was closed, and the staff started looking for a new location. This they found at the site of the Jesuit College at Boulogne, an old

Canadians who have received "blighty wounds" being placed on Ambulance at advanced Dressing Station. June, 1917. (Public Archives of Canada, PA 1404)

college partially destroyed during the French Revolution. The buildings were used for the hospital and huts were erected for the patients. The hospital eventually covered 26 acres of grounds. In January 1916 a 1,560-bed hospital, which could expand to 2,000 in a crisis, was prepared and was ready for operation in February.

* * *

On 8 Dec. 1915 *Punch* published *In Flanders Fields*, anonymously, though the index of that year attributed authorship to McCrae. This poem was the most popular English poem of the Great War. In 1915 there was intense hatred of Germany in England, fuelled by the *Lusitania* sinking, the Zeppelin raids, the use of poison gas, and the atrocity stories. People felt that a long suspected German barbarism had finally revealed itself. McCrae's immensely popular poem did much to encourage the British in the need to defeat the Germans and to avenge the increasing and staggering numbers of British war dead, soldiers and civilians alike. His poem made the poppy, the symbol of oblivion, inseparable from the experience of the First World War. The poem gave "expression to a mood which at the time was universal, and will remain as a permanent record when the mood is passed away."[8]

The poem has McCrae's usual themes of death bringing peace after struggle, and of the voice from the grave; it echoes his 1906 poem *The unconquered dead*. It was the ferocious last third of the poem, so different from the rest, which was used extensively to further the war effort — for recruiting, raising money, attacking both pacifists and profiteers, and comforting the relatives of the dead. It also was a useful piece of propaganda in the Canadian general election of 1917. Together with Rupert Brooke's *The soldier* (1914), Julian Grenfell's *Into battle* (1915), and Laurence Binyoun's *For the fallen* (1914), it was one of the most quoted poems of the war, and of these poems it was the most popular. All were poems written before the monstrous slaughter of the war turned the poetry of the fighting soldiers to bitterness, disillusion, anger, pity, or escapism.

Everyone in the English-speaking world knew the poem. Canadians, especially McCrae's Montreal friends, were proud. Leacock wrote later that "to us in Canada it is a wonderful thought that Jack McCrae's verses and memory should now become part of the common heritage of the English people. These are works of Empire indeed."[9] The poem was especially popular in the United States when she entered the war, and it made McCrae's a household name, albeit a frequently misspelt one.

The poem was printed extensively in the United States usually with one of the better of the 'replies,' that of R.W. Lillard:

Rest ye in peace, ye Flanders dead,
The fight that you so bravely led
We're taken up. And we will keep
True faith with you who lie asleep.
With each a cross to mark his bed,
And poppies blowing overhead,
When once his own life blood ran red;
So let your rest be sweet and deep
    In Flanders Fields

Fear not that you have died for naught,
The torch ye threw to us we caught;
Ten million hands will hold it high
And Freedom's light shall never die!
We learned the lesson that ye taught
    In Flanders Fields.

McCrae received many requests to use *In Flanders Fields* for raising money for the cause. He was sent translations in many languages, including Latin *In agro belgico* ("it needs only Chinese now, surely," said McCrae.) He was modest about its success; his mother sent him clippings about its use and effect. "I return the clippings. I would like to believe them if I dared. I wish they would get to printing 'In F.F.' correctly: it never is nowadays."[10] Apart from seeing his name misspelt, McCrae was surprised to discover the variety of his ranks. "I am promoted Captain this time (Lt. previously)."[11] He was sometimes amused by the response. "Tom sent me some bunk from *The Herald* about me as a 'Guelph boy.' I would fain remind *The Herald* of one or two things in its history — not least the Guelph Junction Railway Bill."[12]

The success of the poem, together with McCrae's early recruitment into the army and his courage at the battle of Ypres, made him a hero to his friends, to the Canadian army, and within the hospital. As for McCrae himself, he was satisfied if the poem enabled men to see where their duty lay.

Officers of Number 3 Canadian General Hospital (McGill) at Boulogne;
John McCrae third from right, front row. (McCrae Birthplace Museum)

CHAPTER THIRTEEN
BOULOGNE: 1916-1918

McCrae's health was undermined by the battles he had been through, although his letters gave little inkling of a change in his temperament caused by the death of his friends, the suffering and waste he saw in the hospital, and the failure to win the war.

Macphail wrote of the change in McCrae:

> After his experience at the front the old gaiety never returned. There were moments of irrascibility and moods of irritation. The desire for solitude grew upon him, and with Bonfire and Bonneau he would go apart for long afternoons far afield by the roads and lanes about Boulogne. The truth is: he felt that he and all had failed and that the torch was thrown from failing hands. We have heard much of the suffering, the misery, the cold, the wet, the gloom of those first three winters; but no tongue has yet uttered the inner misery of heart that was bred of those three years of failure to break the enemy's forces.
>
> He was not alone, in this shadow of deep darkness. Givenchy, Festubert, Neuve-Chapelle, Ypres, Hooge, the Somme — to mention alone the battles in which up to that time the Canadian Corps had been engaged — all ended in failure; and to a sensitive and foreboding mind there were sounds and signs that it would be given to this generation to hear the pillars and fabric of Empire come crashing into the abysm of chaos. He was not at the Somme in that October of 1916, but those who returned up north with the remnants of their division from that place of slaughter will remember that, having done all men could do, they felt like deserters because they had not left their poor bodies dead upon the field along with friends of a lifetime, comrades of a campaign. This is no mere matter of surmise. The last day I spent with him we talked of those things in his tent, and I testify that it is true.[1]

Adami wrote later:

> He felt the war intensely, and it had changed him. Loyal and straightforward as ever, he was no longer the cheery, light-hearted companion of good sayings.... Now, the war was with him night and day, and while kindly and devoted to those under him, he expected from them the same military spirit and sense of high responsibility, and was impatient when he thought either lacking. Not all at first understood the change or could rise to his level of service.[2]

The dreadful impact of the slaughter of his friends with half his brigade at the second battle of Ypres and the anxiety caused by that fight exhausted McCrae; he never recovered. He felt that he should have made greater sacrifices, and insisted on living in a tent through the year, like his comrades at the front, rather than in the officers' huts. When this affected his health in mid-winter he had to be ordered into warmer surroundings. To many he gave the impression that he felt he should still be with his old artillery brigade. After the battle of Ypres he was never again the optimistic man with the infectious smile. His friends spoke of his change of temperament in subdued voices, feeling, as one said, that an icon had been broken.

McCrae rarely took leave. His relaxations were long, melancholy rides on Bonfire through the Boulogne countryside, with the dog Bonneau trotting by his side, and his reading and letter writing. He should probably have been sent back to Canada to lighter duties, but the need for doctors was too great and he would not have agreed to return. For him the war had to be won; he could not break faith with the dead of Flanders. The message of *In Flanders Fields* was uncompromising.

McCrae's twice-weekly letters to his mother from 1916 to 1918 record his life at the hospital and give his comments on the war. He wrote of his close companionship with his horse, Bonfire, and his dog, Bonneau. It was said of McCrae that children and animals followed him as shadows other men, and his love of his horse and dog, and of other dogs he encountered, increased with his desire for solitude. He wrote "I have a very deep affection for Bonfire, for we have been through so much together, and some of it bad enough. All the hard spots to which one's memory turns the old fellow has shared, though he says so little about it."[3] McCrae wrote often to his friends — Oskar Klotz, the Archibalds, Maude Abbott, 'Charley' Martin, and Lord Grey; and as the war dragged on his letters became more affectionate.

The tent in which McCrae lived was impossible to keep dry in January and February of 1916. In February the tent doors and everything damp inside were frozen solid — yet he still took a cold bath in the mornings.

The hospital started admitting patients in mid February 1916. It was hampered in its work by the lack, and the high turnover, of officers. Another complaint of McCrae concerned the Sisters, who were otherwise splendid: "their training leads them to want to do less in a perfect way, and we want more in a less perfect way, because it is war." To his mother he wrote:

> My duties are so multifarious that I find it hard to get them done. So much to do outside the professional work, for the adjutant's work (alas! without his pay) falls entirely upon me, and everybody comes to me with their squeals and their complaints. The nursing sisters are hard to suit — they think everything should be right before anything can be done, and some do not realize that things have to be done the best ways one can, or even undone.
>
> One got to Colonel Elder — 'If that is the case we might as well dig our own graves!'
>
> 'Isn't that what you came for' was his terse and not unpertinent reply.

John McCrae on "Bonfire", Boulogne 1916-1917. (McCrae Birthplace Museum)

He thought it would do a lot of the hospital staff

> good to have a week at the front. One NCO was away temporarily, and came back rather scandalized: they made him sleep in a hay-loft! I have not vast pity for them. Life is quiet and perhaps even dull, but cheerfulness is a duty and we must try to perform it.

In March 1916 went on leave in London, staying with his cousin Walter Gow and visiting the Oslers at Oxford. Norman Gwyn from Number 1 Canadian General Hospital was staying there with his sister, Nona Gwyn, who was in Oxford for much of the war. As already indicated there is a story that McCrae broke off an engagement to Nona Gwyn in 1917. Whatever the truth, McCrae never mentioned Nona in his letters to his mother. Lady Osler wrote that McCrae had proposed to Nona Gwyn in Scotland in 1914 but had been turned down by her then.[4] This was possibly on the grounds that McCrae would not marry her until the war was over since Lady Osler wrote elsewhere that "it seems a shame that his peculiar ideas should have prevented their being happy."[5] Since Lady Osler also wrote that McCrae had always hoped that Nona Gwyn would relent it is uncertain whether there was indeed an engagement.

McCrae was clear that his duty lay with the war. He enjoyed his leave greatly, particularly the solid sleep so rare in France. He returned in early April.

In April 1916 the hospital took in increased numbers of Canadians, the corps then being in the Ypres Salient. Colonel David McCrae, John McCrae's father, had raised a regiment in Guelph, the 43rd Battery, C.E.F., but, being 73 years old, was not allowed to leave England for France and was ordered home. John was given special leave of three days in London to see him in May, and with some reluctance left for Boulogne. While in London, McCrae saw Sir Max Aitken and General Watson to try to get his father over to France, even

Bringing Canadian wounded to the Field Dressing Station, Vimy Ridge, April 1917. Photograph taken during the Battle of Vimy Ridge. (Public Archives of Canada, PA 1024)

for a week, so that when he returned to Canada David McCrae could better help recruiting. He failed to gain his authorization, but his father did pay a brief visit to France.

In early June the German successes at Mount Sorrel resulted in the arrival of numerous convoys of patients, including many Canadians, at the hospital. Thanks to the Canadians, the German successes were reversed. Although kept short of artillery by Haig, who was preparing for the Somme battles, they attacked on 13 June, and recaptured their old line. It was the first clear-cut victory of the war, and was partly the result of new tactics used — a night attack, a smoke screen, and good artillery support. The cost in men was high, however, and convoys arrived day and night for a week at Number 3 Canadian General Hospital, bringing 1,000 men of the 1st Canadian Division.

On 30 June the hospital was ordered to "evacuate to England all patients who could live to get there ... (and as) great events implied endless casualties, the staff ... prepared to meet whatever demand the situation should present."[6] On 1 July 1916 the battle of the Somme started. Since February the Germans had been destroying the French army at Verdun in the first of the battles of attrition. Meanwhile General Haig was preparing for the "Great Offensive" on the Somme, the decisive blow to end the war. The site was chosen because here the French and British lines met. The British general staff were intoxicated with confidence; 750,000 Allied men were involved in the preparations, and five cavalry divisions awaited the breakthrough. The general staff had complete confidence that, after the greatest artillery bombardment in history, "nothing could exist at the conclusion ... in the area covered by it." Reports that the German double-line of 30-yard-thick wire was not cut, nor the machine guns silenced, were regarded by them as evidence of 'funk.'

On 1 July, in broad daylight, 100,000 of Kitchener's new volunteer army attacked on an 18-mile front. Waves of heavily-laden British infantry rose from their trenches and walked shoulder to shoulder in well-dressed lines into the machine gun bullets. At the end of the first day of the "Great Offensive," 20,000 British soldiers were dead and 40,000 lay wounded. The war poet Edmund Blunden later wrote: "By the end of the day, both sides had seen, in a sad scrawl of broken earth and murdered men, the answer to the question. No road. No thoroughfare. Neither race had won, nor could win, the War. The War had won, and would go on winning."[7]

In July the resources of Number 3 Canadian General Hospital were strained by the procession of convoys and evacuations — 4,600 men in the first two weeks, with 670 men on 21 July alone. In August there was a momentary lull in the fighting, but the September fighting again increased the hospital's intake.

McCrae recorded this period in a letter to his mother on 23 July, 1916:
Busy time — I less than most, as I refuse to keep a dog and bark myself. My job is the selected cases and to see that the work is done. I really see a good many each day.... Entertained a dozen members of the Parliamentary Commission or something — we gave them the best

113

dinner we could scrape; for my own part I sat between G.E. Foster, and Sen. Landry and had a very dull time. Sir George spoke of the 'injudicious things that had been said by the people and newspapers to irritate the Germans living in Canada.' Grrrrr!!! I told what I thought about that, and about peace terms to any German!! (A kind of waste — the visit.)"

And on 30 July, 1916: "Heavy work. See 30-40 people as 'consultant' per day. Streak of ill-luck in our lung wards, which are my province. But before, we had been very fortunate, so perhaps it is just evening up."

The battle went on for 2½ months with 500,000 British casualties, the best of a generation and Britain's future squandered by Haig and his staff. The Canadian corps was involved in September and November, 77,000 Canadians advancing 3,000 yards for a loss of 24,000 men. The number of men fighting in the Somme on both sides in 1916 was 3,000,000 with 1,000,000 casualties, of which nearly half were British.

In many of his letters of this period McCrae talked of the sameness of the days, the lack of change or excitement, and the absence of leave, although "I have a deeply rooted objection to leave while my job lasts." Everyone else took leave. He read much — books about the war and light fiction. He disliked bureaucracy.

Colonel Birkett is a great man for filing, while if I had my way I would basket a great deal of it.

I need an office as much as an elephant needs sidepockets, but it is forced upon me. I use it to write my letters; but that is about all. I refuse to keep files of military communications. The Colonel loves correspondence and files, and I detest them. Col. Elder and I saved a lot of energy when we ran the hospital; and seemed to get on well enough.

McCrae had few expenses. His mother and friends deluged him with socks and tobacco. Throughout the war he bought War Loans with his pay, accumulating several thousands of dollars. In October he wrote to his mother:

It is wonderful to think of the punishment we have taken, and it makes one proud to think that we could take it: I think the world will find that nothing in our lifetime has ever given us reason to suspect what John Bull can be; we think he is frivolously chivalrous, and forgiving, but I think if Germany counts on that she is due for a second think. I think and trust that Great Britain is going to be the most exacting of all. Words ... fail me to describe how I hate Germany and the UnGermans, and there are probably some others.

Recurring asthma in October persuaded McCrae to move indoors from his tent and he slept better. "I have the usual awful bark that is as bad as whooping cough while it lasts." It did not improve, and in November pleurisy and bronchitis forced him to a hospital for officers at Wimereux. Treated by his friend Sir Bertrand Dawson, the king's physician, he spent 10 days in bed and

John McCrae and his dog Bonneau. (Public Archives of Canada, C 46284)

then was sent to a convalescent hotel on the Riviera, near Monte Carlo, where he was soon bored. He returned much improved to Boulogne.

The last six months of 1916 were a time of controversy concerning the Canadian medical services in England. As might be expected, Sir Sam Hughes was responsible. The bitterness and distrust generated by the affair remained strong in Canada and in the army throughout the rest of the war. According to Macphail's *Official history of the medical services*:

> The medical service was selected by the minister as the ground for his struggle for control of the army. Upon that field he fell.... This proposal to segregate Canadians in Canadian hospitals was the immediate incident which caused the extrusion of the Minister from the Cabinet. In itself it must appear inadequate. The further explanation is that the measure was part of his general policy to segregate as completely as possible the whole Canadian Corps from the British Expeditionary Force.

115

The facts were these. In July 1916 Hughes appointed Colonel Bruce to report on the Canadian Medical Services. Bruce's report was critical of a number of practices, and recommended that all Canadian wounded and sick be treated only in Canadian hospitals, a physical impossibility. The director of medical services, General Carleton Jones, was sacked, and Bruce installed in his place; in protest Sir William Osler and J.G. Adami resigned their posts as consultants. A further committee, the Babtie Committee, castigated Bruce's report as unjust and undeserved. Hughes was forced to resign, to the army's great satisfaction.

In his letters McCrae described his disgust at Hughes, Colonel Bruce, and the Canadian medical service in England. He disliked politicians and wrote in July 1917:

> Walter (Gow) was here two days ago — a very welcome visitor ... he stayed to lunch. His guide was Captain Rogers — a stupid looking man (son of Bob Rogers — politician) who has been in the army since Jan '17 and who has been over the Italian front and the British front. Why don't they let someone with brains see the war, instead of their useless political pets.

In September 1917:

> I hear that Simpson, one of the Western crowd, having been whitewashed, is to be sent back to command a hospital, which is decidedly hard on the hospital, I must say, and on those who are in it. As he was arrested there, they want to give him rehabilitation, I suppose. But how disgusting to use the service to rehabilitate discredited political hacks; still, it is very Canadian, at the present time. At times, I find it hard to be proud of my citizenship.

McCrae objected to the popular kind of religion which was preached by the chaplains and which for him was typified by the hymns chosen for the soldiers. Surrounded by the questions and contradictions raised by war, sudden death, and squalid living, the average bluff, genial, sporty Church of England chaplain was revealed to be the amateur he was. Some of McCrae's letters describe his reaction.

> The Padre nearly got on ticklish ground when he was getting near the statement that we may not hate the Germans. (4 April, 1916)
> The Service was taken by a YMCA man who is said to be a 'Con. Objector,' so I am not sure that I would have felt very 'called' anyway." (22 October, 1916)
> At Church tonight with the Presbyterian parson conducting. At times I get past words. Tonight a hymn with the chorus 'Jesus saves! Jesus saves!' and another with the line 'Praise the Mount — I'm fixed upon it' which sounds to me like a guffaw at a funeral. It is queer how relatively careless some of the Padres are with hymns. The service ended with

'Abide with me' and the way the men sang it would tell anybody not to tinker with the drivel that too often passes as praise. (*18 April, 1917*)

Church this evening of the C of E persuasion: the Presbyterian service this a.m.: I am glad that I had not gone when, passing the hut, I heard the strains of 'Throw out the Lifeline.' I have hinted strongly to the Padre that such stuff is probably popular with no one, but he holds on at the same course. (*25 March, 1917*)

We have *six* padres at the moment: isn't it ridiculous? We are really a boarding house for them. (*1 July, 1917*)

At Church this evening: it was a pleasant service: but our padre will dwell on the fact that we have brought this on ourselves and as soon as we as a nation assume the right devotional attitude — peace will come with a rush. There are theological pitfalls these days, I am afraid, as in the past. (*19 August, 1917*)

A new Padre! (*16 December, 1917*)

Staff of Number 3 Canadian General Hospital (McGill) parading in the grounds of the ruined Jesuit College, Boulogne. (From "Number 3 Canadian General Hospital (McGill), 1914-1919" by R.C. Fetherstonhaugh. Montreal: Gazette Publishing Company)

In late 1916 President Wilson of the United States tried to persuade the parties to the war to state, once and for all, what they were fighting for. There was virulent condemnation by all the warring nations. McCrae called him an ass, writing that "we have come as near as we can to destroying Germany, as at present constituted," and quoted Morrison, now commander of the Second Canadian Division Artillery, as saying that after the artillery fire in one of the Somme battles " 'I saw so many dead Germans that I was satisfied' — which says a good deal in the mouth of that little fire eater."

After 1916 there was no possibility of peace. Too much blood had been shed and too much hatred released for there to be any outcome but costly victory for one side or the other. The disappointments of 1916 showed that no side could win clear-cut victory, that both sides were exhausted, and that further battles of attrition would continue to wear down both armies. The politicians knew the generals to be bankrupt, the generals thought the politicians to be meddling, the public blamed all the leaders. There was uncertainty and disillusion, but for most of the British one thing was clear — the war had to be won. In the front line most men saw "that it was up to them to pull the foundered rulers of England and heads of the army through the scrape."[8] After the war England's diseases might be surgically cured — but "you could not change the fire-brigade while there was a fire on."[9] McCrae was more optimistic than most about the progress of the war. In Canada the flamboyant pride of the English in the empire had taken stunning blows, but the dominant mood was to see the fight through to victory, not to break faith with the dead of Flanders. In Canada it was said that McCrae's *In Flanders Fields* did "more for civilian morale than any other written or spoken contribution to the cause."[10]

In early 1917 British morale on the western front was low, and made worse by an extremely cold January; in early February McCrae had returned to sleeping in his tent. He wrote in several letters:

I have never suffered so from cold in my life ... the oldest inhabitant, who is a notorious liar of course, is quite out of the game: it is beyond his experience. 20 degrees below zero. Centigrade.... To go to bed is a nightmare and to get up a worse one.... I was never so tired of anything in my life. One feels a kind of blind anger which one cannot vent upon anyone; no riding, 1,400 patients.... frost on the floor of the buildings.... sad lot of serious pneumonias and I am very tired of it.

In 1917 there were indications that the outlook would improve for the Allies. The United States was still neutral despite provocation since the sinking of the *Lusitania*, but there were signs that she would declare war. McCrae wrote in January: "It seems as if Germany's own mother will have difficulty recognising her, if things go as they appear to be going. There will be busy times in the spring." But in March nothing had happened and he wrote that "it is strange to see the U.S. as blind today as we were in 1914."

In April the United States entered the war. This advantage to the Allies was offset by the Russian Revolution in March. The final collapse of that country in August meant that German troops could be transferred to the west in time for the battle of Passchendaele. Allied prospects dimmed seriously in late 1917.

In the early months of 1917 work at the hospital continued steadily. One of the irritations to McCrae was the continued stream of visitors — "we find this a great place for visitors, we call it a blank hotel: every Canadian that comes through seems to drop in.... Am I getting less gregarious in my old age? I suppose so."

McCrae had to entertain visitors ranging from officers of the Japanese Imperial Medical Service to Prime Minister Borden of Canada, "a form of duty which makes me very tired." Another problem was the high turnover of young officers. "Today we have 10 junior officers thrown in on us: they clutter up the mess room, which is our only home, and we do not need them: they will doubtless be redistributed in a day or two." Later in the year he wrote:

> "(Politicians) make me rather sick: we see a great many of them here spending the country's money for ---- what! no-body knows most of the time.... Only 2 of 9 new officers know their business — so my rounds are rather tiresome affairs these days.

McCrae recorded his life in those early months of 1917 as dull and quiet; he was becoming crusty and stale. In early April he had leave in London, and saw his cousin Walter Gow, J.G. Adami, and the Oslers. He returned refreshed, in time to receive some of the casualties of the battle of Vimy Ridge. The battle was a spectacular success, with excellent use of artillery by E.W.B. Morrison, and good planning by the Canadian Corps Staff. The Canadians advanced the line 2½ miles and took 4,000 prisoners for a loss of 10,000 men. For the Allies it was a thrilling victory: 9 April, 1917 has been called "the day Canada became a nation." The victory was offset, however, by losses in further fighting and later by the failure of the French on the Aisne. By midsummer the French army had collapsed in mutiny and was no longer a fighting force. The war of attrition had bled the French too much; by the end of the war half of all French men between 18 and 36 years old were dead. It was the loss of the French and Russian armies and the failures of the British in the autumn fighting which was to cause the Allies so much anxiety in 1917; the only hope of victory lay with the American army, which would not be effective until 1918.

In May 1917 McCrae wrote to his mother:

Queen Mary visits Number 3 Canadian General Hospital, McCrae on her right. (McCrae Birthplace Museum)

Do you see that Britain is paying the Duchess of Saxe Coburg Gotha 6000 pounds a year? She lives in Germany and has a son in the German army. Something more to thank our dear old Queen Victoria for, besides the Albert Memorial and the Lake Poets. Verily, we are a d.f. nation in some ways.... I did not go to the Kirk today: not entirely that I was afraid of the chorus   hymns, but they lessen the regret.

In early June a spectacular British victory at Messines came as a badly needed tonic after the depressing end of the British and French spring offensives. Unlike the other British attacks, it adopted the tactics of siege-warfare, exploding 19 mines planted with 600 tons of explosives under the German lines. The British advanced 2½ miles for a loss of only 16,000 casualties, increasing the width of the Ypres Salient.

On 30 June 1917 McCrae's poem *The anxious dead* was published in the

English weekly magazine the *Spectator*. He had written it at the end of 1916 but wrote to his mother that he thought it would fit very well the Messines-Ypres advance. Publication of the poem in the *Spectator* was a "long cherished ambition."

The anxious dead

O Guns, fall silent till the dead men hear
Above their heads the legions pressing
    on:
(These fought their fight in time of bitter fear,
And died not knowing how the day had gone.)

O flashing muzzles, pause, and let them see
    The coming dawn that streaks the sky afar;
Then let your mighty chorus witness be
    To them, and Caesar, that we still make war.

Tell them, O guns, that we have heard their call,
    that we have sworn, and will not turn aside,
That we will onward till we win or fall,
    That we will keep the faith for which they
        died.

Bid them be patient, and some day, anon,
    They shall feel earth enwrapt in silence deep;
Shall greet, in wonderment, the quiet dawn,
    And in content may turn them to their sleep.

The poem did not capture the British imagination as *In Flanders Fields* had, though it was widely quoted at the time. It achieved some fame when quoted by Sir Edward Carsons in London at a meeting to raise money for the Ulster soldiers' charities, and the *London News* had a drawing on the centre page headed by one of the poem's lines. McCrae commented that it "will hardly go as far as Flanders Fields, I think." It lacked the recruiting poster rhetoric.

123

In July the Germans started using a new type of poison gas, "Mustard Gas," and by the end of the month the hospital had 300 cases. In late July the preparations for the third battle of Ypres began, a battle which was to continue for the rest of the summer and to end in the swamps of Passchendaele. The Germans, warned by the Allied success at Messine, changed their defence tactics and the enormous British artillery shelling, firing 4¾ tons of explosive per yard of front, served only to warn the enemy and destroy the ground over which the British would attack. The military lessons of the war had not been learned by the general staff and the war of attrition dragged on. Criticism of the British general staff was bitter throughout the army, and the early optimism of the summer faded as men prepared for another winter. Throughout the summer casualties from third Ypres poured steadily into McCrae's hospital, though with the increasing surgery and treatment in the front-line areas there was a progressive improvement in the condition of the wounded arriving in Boulogne. In the first four weeks of the battle of Passchendaele the British advanced two miles on a front of several thousand yards, for a loss of 68,000 men. By October, when the Canadian corps was committed to the fighting, 51 of the total 60 British divisions in France were fighting in the Ypres Salient. Ypres and the villages around had virtually disappeared. The fighting ended in November when the Canadians captured Passchendaele. The offensive lasted 109 days, deepened the Ypres Salient 4½ miles, and cost 300,000 Allied casualties.

The Canadians were now generally regarded as "shock troops" by the Germans and the British, since they had proved their worth in the few "victories" of the war. The success of the Canadians was due to their national spirit, to their commanders, and to the moral and physical strength of the men. As some Canadian imperialists had realized long before the war, the excesses of the industrial revolution and of the English class system had had serious effects on the average Englishman. There was a striking contrast between the "battalions of colourless, stunted, half-toothless lads from hot, humid Lancashire mills; battalions of slow, staring faces, gargoyles out of the tragical-comical-historical-pastoral edifice of modern English rural life" and the "Dominion battalions of men startlingly taller, stronger, handsomer, prouder, firmer in nerve, better schooled, more boldly interested in life."[10]

But the war needed an "endless stream of men, men, men, limbers, men, mules, guns, men (who took) months to train, seconds to kill."[11] In Canada the supply was drying up, in part because of disillusion with the losses which the British generalship had allowed at the Somme, Arras, and Passchendaele. It was almost universally believed in English Canada that Britain's cause was just, but by 1916 recruitment was virtually nil in Quebec and declining in the rest of Canada. In April and May 1917 only 3,000 men volunteered for the army although in the same months there were 20,000 Canadian casualties in France. Borden decided to bring in conscription and a Military Service Bill was introduced to Parliament in June 1917. Liberal leader Sir Wilfred Laurier declined to support this bill unless there was an election, which was held in

December 1917. Resentment in Quebec was high, though in other provinces most people supported conscription. As in the Boer War, the country was again split along cultural lines. The political wrangling over conscription lasted many months. The Germans were also anxiously watching the outcome of the conscription issue in Canada; the Australian army had voted against it.

McCrae's letters contained statements like the following:

> I see with inexpressible disgust the talk of an election in Canada; if Laurier lets it go on, it is the Fr. Canadian coming out, and I promise him he will never have a vote of mine. We don't want this party foolishness interfering with the war.... I do not expect to mince my ideas about the Fr. Canadians for the rest of my days.... What a lot of muckers there are in our parliamentary and other circles. I don't admire the last appearance of the Pope (bearing peace proposals) very much or of his representatives in Canada on the conscription question. We had old Begin (Archbishop of Quebec) here and the authorities made a fuss over him and ran him around. And now I see that he turns around like a true son of his Church. *Bah!*

In December the country and the army voted in a heavily gerrymandered election, which was marked by the enfranchisement of all close female relatives of servicemen, living or dead. The country, except Quebec, voted overwhelmingly for conscription. It was said that *"In Flanders Fields* did more to make this Dominion persevere in the duty of fighting for the world's ultimate peace than all the political speeches of the recent campaign."[12] McCrae wrote that "I hope I stabbed a Fr. Canadian with my vote" ... and that "Bourassa ought to be in prison or dead at the hands of the law." He was highly pleased with the election results.

(McCrae Birthplace Museum)

125

In 1917 the first Victory Loan Bonds were floated in Canada, using lines from *In Flanders Fields* to advertise them; designed to raise $150,000,000, they raised $400,000,000.

In the late summer and autumn of 1917 the hospital continued to treat the wounded from the slaughter at Passchendaele. Among those killed in the autumn was Revere Osler, an indescribably "bitter blow to his parents, poor people." Sir William, haunted so long by fears of Revere's death, wrote: "Dear laddie! he loathed the whole business of war, and I dare say is glad to be at peace out of the hell of the past 6 months."[13]

In the autumn of 1917 Colonel Birkett, the officer commanding the hospital, was invalided to England, and Colonel Elder was appointed to replace him. McCrae thought this appointment unfair, since he was senior to Elder. He felt that he should have been given the command, which would have included a promotion in army rank. In early 1916 he had nearly been "Mentioned in Despatches" but refused the honour since "I have a feeling that the despatches ought to be for the front and that lines of communications should get some other form of recognition." McCrae recorded an "inclination to envy" later on when his friends received decorations. When he asked why Colonel Elder was to receive the command he was told it was because Elder was soon going home and had served a long time without recognition. Elder had also served on the Babtie Committee which reported on Colonel Bruce's report, and in this capacity may have made an impression on the Canadian Army Medical authorities. McCrae, though he did not want the responsibility of commanding, wrote: "... as if I were not equally deserving, and with less recognition, and a good many years senior. I do not like to have it put over me." In October he went to London where he saw Adami, Macphail, and the director-general of medical services, General G.L. Foster, about the problem. Foster countered his seniority argument by saying that seniority referred to service in the C.A.M.C. and not just the army. To Edward Archibald, McCrae wrote:

> I told the General that I thought it was D--- hard that E's recognition had to be at my expense. His claim was that I am a mere youth (in the CAMC so's Elder, by the way) and that my undoubted seniority to E. is merely a catch vote so to speak. I told the Gen. I did not think they should do it, because if it is those grounds I qualify on them even before Elder does. We have talked it out quite amicably here (with Elder) and there will be no trouble whatever. But isn't it an official way of doing things? I told Gen. F. they needn't be squeamish about making E. a Colonel: they had made lots of Colonels out of nothing before this, let alone a good man.[14]

To his mother he wrote of his disappointment at not being promoted and attributed it to

> low-down wire pulling. If I would stoop to it I have no doubt Walter (Gow — deputy minister of overseas military forces of Canada) and Gen. Turner would nail the whole business flat as a pancake, but I would scorn to use such methods. I always said there were too many female

126

*Officer's Mess, Number 3 Canadian General Hospital (McGill),
Boulogne, 1916-1917. (From "Number 3 General Hospital (McGill),
1914-1919" by R.C. Fetherstonhaugh. Montreal: Gazette Publishing
Company.)*

relatives in England and this confirms it. Well, confound the whole dirty
business anyway. It is a real Canadian way of doing things.

In April 1917 the first Portuguese patients and doctors had arrived at the
hospital, their country having recently entered the war on the side of the Allies.
They were to annoy the Canadian hospital for the rest of the war. The presence
of six Portuguese officers in the mess, McCrae wrote, "strikes as a kind of stick
... their men steal everything." In January 1918 large numbers of Portuguese
patients arrived. McCrae wrote then:

Our 'oldest allies' are still crowding the wards, and we are getting more
and more 'fed up' with them; but it will be a long time yet before they get
their own hospital built. The present arrangement suits them so well: we

127

have to forego our professional control over them, and we have also withdrawn their results from our statistics. Obviously.

In late 1917 there was widespread feeling in the army that a negotiated peace was possible, and that failing such a peace the war could last 20 years or longer. Siegfried Sassoon, the widely-read war poet, made a statement to the press:

I believe that this war, upon which I entered as a war of defence and liberation, has now become a war of aggression and conquest. I believe that the purpose for which I and my fellow-soldiers entered upon this war should have been so clearly stated as to make it impossible to change them, and that, had this been done, the objects which actuated us would now be attainable by negotiation.

In a slightly different vein, Lord Lansdowne, the ex-foreign secretary, published his well-known letter suggesting that a meaningful victory was no longer possible. He asked: "Can we afford to go on paying the same sort of price for the same sort of gains ... Let our naval, military and economic advisers tell us frankly whether they are satisfied that the knock-out blow can be delivered." McCrae's response was: "What a silly old ass Lansdowne made of himself. I never had much use for him — I always thought of him a politician rather than a statesman."

By Christmas 1917 army morale was low; the Allies were realizing both the extent and consequence of the Russian collapse. German reinforcements from the east were, for the first time in the war, bringing their numbers on the western front above those of the Allies.

McCrae's health had been poor all summer. In August he recorded that he was "tied by the heels for the last couple of days with the old enemy — a real snorter of an attack, beginning for no reason that I could see," and his asthmatic attacks stayed with him, possibly exacerbated by the effects of chlorine gas inhaled at the battle of Ypres. Many who saw him that summer recorded the change in his temperament; one friend described him in early 1918 as "silent, asthmatic, moody."[15]

On 24 January 1918 McCrae was appointed consulting physician to the First British Army — the first Canadian so honoured. McCrae was pleased when Elder told him but he had been ill in bed for a day, and stayed there. On the afternoon of the 24th he reported that he was developing pneumonia. Sir Bertrand Dawson examined him but could find no signs of pneumonia, although a stain of sputum showed the presence of bacteria. The next day McCrae was moved to Number 14 British General Hospital for Officers. He appeared better but was worried about himself and said he knew it was the end. On the 26th there was evidence of meningitis, and he lost consciousness. He died at 1:30 a.m. on 28 January 1918.

The news spread rapidly, and messages of regret poured into the hospital. "Number 3 had been proud of him and shared the army's delight in *In Flanders Fields* and *The Anxious Dead*, and admired his keen professional skill. No man had toiled more selflessly in the service of those committed to his care."[16] His many friends were broken-hearted, in part because he became unconscious so quickly that they could not see him; one nurse wrote that "he has gone never knowing how much we cared."[17]

McCrae was buried with full military honours two days later in the cemetery at Wimereux. His friends were there — E.W.B. Morrison and W.O.H. Dodds from the artillery; Sir Arthur Currie, the Canadian corps commander; Sir Almroth Wright; Harvey Cushing and the Harvard Unit; Sir Bernard Dawson; and the staff of Number 3 Canadian General Hospital. Bonfire led the procession, with McCrae's riding boots reversed in the stirrups. The burial service was conducted by Canon Almond, an old friend from Montreal and from his artillery brigade.

McCrae's funeral about to move off from Number 14 British Officer's Hospital, Boulogne, 29 January 1918. (Public Archives of Canada, C 18550)

Elder wrote:
The day of the funeral was a beautiful spring day; none of us wore overcoats. You know the haze that comes over the hills at Wimereux. I felt so thankful that the poet of 'Flanders Fields' was lying out there in the bright sunshine in the open space he loved so well, instead of being cramped in that miserable city graveyard which he hated so much.[18]

Tank in badly shelled mud area. Battle of Passchendaele, November 1917. (Public Archives of Canada, PA 2195)

On Armistice Day, 11 November 1918, the day that Germany surrendered to the Allies, a long-serving member of the 1st Brigade Canadian Field Artillery wrote to his mother a letter which captures what *In Flanders Fields* meant to so many of the fighting men. The letter also shows the spirit required to ensure that Allied soldiers kept faith with their dead in Flanders. For them the war had to be won; that such a war must never be repeated was clear.

Just a few words, but I couldn't let today go by without writing.

I can't believe it ... but the end has come; no more horror or death or fear, for peace has come.

On the whole line at eleven o'clock this morning, the 'cease fire' was passed along, and not till then.... The great game was played out and the job done. Not by diplomacy or wrangling — but by sheer brutal force of arms, and after the most terrible continued pressure any army ever felt, the enemy has gone down....

And what have we seen? Good heaven, it is like a dream, old mother, and may this world never see another like it again....

When I think of the friends who lie in the battered fields and graveyards of this land, I don't think we can split on anything again. We will all go back to our homes and our people, but we will never forget them....

There is Lex Helmer up hard by the Yser Canal, Lim Pearson in the battered churchyard of Bailleux, Smith beside the Ancre, one Paddy Waters by the Canal du Nord, and poor old Ray with his torn and twisted gunwheel only five short miles away — the last battle. Good men and true, all of them, and thank Christ we who are left did not let them die in vain. They can all sleep happy, for the work is done.

And if France ever fights for life again, I hope to God we are there to help, for we are part of this country and have paid a high price. Mother, some day I would love to bring you through France and show you what she has suffered, and the little corners where we have lost so many men we can ill spare. I only hope all mankind has learned the hellishness of war.

Why I am alive I do not know. I never deserved to live while so many truer men went down, but all I can say is that my spirit has been willing to go. The flesh has been weak, at times, very weak, but my spirit has never been afraid to pay the price if I had been called.

And now, old lover, I must go. I will come back dear, to you all, and for God's sake love me hard. I'll need it, and I'll be as wild as a hawk, but four years is a long time.

Poppy Day, Canada (?1919). (McCrae Birthplace Museum)

Victory

..."thank Christ we who are left did not let them die in vain"... "Victory."
(McCrae Birthplace Museum)

CHAPTER FOURTEEN
CONCLUSION

Although John McCrae would have felt that he had broken faith had he lived while so many had died, the reaction of his friends and contemporaries to his death in France in 1918 was one of great grief. They wrote of his unswerving fidelity, his professional ability, his many talents, his wide knowledge, his kindliness, and his charm. McCrae was greatly loved by all who knew him, and his contemporaries felt that death had cheated them of the best which was to come. His brother tried to comfort the family by telling them that the bitter and disillusioned man who would have returned from the war was not the sparkling man who went to it.

Had McCrae lived, he would have been proud that the war had given a new pride to Canada and a new identity to her sons in the changed relation with the mother country. From a population of eight million, 620,000 Canadians fought in France, 61,326 were killed, and one-third were wounded — the colonial country rose to nationhood through the courage of her soldiers. McCrae would have been scathing of the Treaty of Versailles, in which the next war was implicit. He would have been pleased that, because of *In Flanders Fields*, the poppy was adopted to remember the war dead of the British empire, and is sold in millions every November 11 around the world. He would have remained grief-stricken by the deaths of so many of his friends and patients but pleased to know that his medical colleagues remembered him in a stained-glass window in Montreal which called him "Pathologist, Poet, Physician, Soldier, a Man among Men."

Before he died McCrae knew his poem to be the most popular of the English-language war verses. It had captured the mood of the British public in 1915. He was pleased by its effects in the empire and in the United States. Its impact was enormous. It was the poem of the British army. It was quoted everywhere — with frenzy in selling war bonds and encouraging recruiting, with conviction in harassing pacifists or pillorying profiteers, and with compassion in comforting the relatives of the myriad war dead. The poem was written by a man who had previously published little poetry and who wrote verse as a form of relaxation. But *In Flanders Fields* has the hallmarks of his other poems — the preoccupation with death, the desire for oblivion, and the voice from the grave.

Modern critics, favouring poets more gifted and more critical of the slaughter have placed McCrae's poem in a quiet corner. The British world was changed irrevocably by the Great War, and *In Flanders Fields* is now an anachronism, to be dusted off for lip-service to dead heroes, or to be learned as an exercise by school children. To understand the poem, the poet, and the circumstances of the writing is to enter a lost world, a world unscarred by the futility of the trenches. It is to know how men felt who volunteered for the War, men who believed that they were fighting evil for the future of mankind. But reality was Passchendaele, Arras, Hill 70, Verdun, Vimy Ridge, The Somme, and other killing grounds. Soldiers do not die without wounds, and McCrae saw it all, from the cheering crowds to the obscenity of corrupted flesh. The War broke his heart.

McCrae was a man of many facets, all undergirded by strong and complementary characteristics of loyalty, service, and duty. These qualities shine through from his early days of effort and expectation, during his middle years of full-blooded vigour, and to the the last days in Flanders of grief, disillusion, and loneliness. He was loved by nearly all who knew him, but stood away from love. The best of company, friend of the great and the near-great, master of anecdote and humour, leaving the impression of continuous laughter, McCrae walked alone. His concern for people — family, students, friends, patients, soldiers — was a marked characteristic. He was a physician of distinction among distinguished physicians, a brave soldier among brave soldiers, and a poet, writer, and artist of no mean achievement. He had a great love for children and animals, with whom he could relax and enjoy a natural affection.

The strong faith of his Presbyterian ancestors is a clue to his character, and the way he made this faith his own is a reflection of his own qualities and achievements. Life could be fun but must also be taken seriously; an account of the use of his talents would be required. Only the best was acceptable, and he required the same high standards of others as he had of himself. Incompetence, medical or military, was not tolerated. He sought the best — in soldiering, medicine, poetry, and his friendships. His Presbyterian upbringing gave him a strong sense of duty while soldiering provided the adventure otherwise missing in the serious and high-minded pattern of his life. The conflict evident in his early poetry, between love of things human and his duty to the Divine, he never resolved. And yet he was not a sad man. He loved life. His smile was infectious.

McCrae's life was a microcosm of the years of tumultuous change through which he lived and which touched him at every point: in medicine, the great advances associated with Pasteur, Lister, and Osler; in the hubristic period of the empire, with Kipling, Strathcona, Milner, and Grey; in the Boer and Great War, the first inklings of the eventual destruction of the empire; in the military, the dedication to attrition associated with French and Haig; in Canada, the sense of national identity linked with participation in the Boer War, the rapid rise in population, and the change from a pioneer to an industrialized country.

Had McCrae survived he might have felt like his old friend Andrew Macphail, who in old age saw himself as a mid-Victorian relic. On Remembrance Day in 1936 Macphail wrote:

> It is now somewhat the fashion to pity them, that they died in vain, and to deride us that we served in vain ... hysterical writings of neurotic

adolescents who should never have been allowed to enlist ... apt to forget the ancient dogma that war is the father of all things, of this city, of this Province, of Canada itself, of the freedom we enjoy, and of our future freedom ... war evolved the best qualities with which man is endowed, fortitude, courage, fidelity in duty, and loyalty to comrades, respect for our enemies, and humanity towards them when they come into our power...."[1]

The conclusion of many younger men was different. They felt that their dead comrades would be betrayed unless a way to prevent future wars was found. Some put their hope in the League of Nations, only to see that body decay within a generation through neglect and the self-interest of the great powers.

The comparison of John McCrae with Norman Bethune, an equally famous Canadian doctor who died serving the Communist revolutionaries in China, is irresistible. Yet the contrast is also striking. McCrae was a late Victorian gentleman and staunch Presbyterian with a strong sense of his duty to serve the poor. He expressed none of Bethune's anger about poverty or about the inequalities in medical care for rich and poor. Bethune's anger was part of the enormous disillusion with the structure of a society which produced the slaughter of the First World War and also the subsequent economic depression of the 1930s. But both McCrae and Bethune, who was also an associate of Edward Archibald, had similarities in their strong sense of honour and honesty, and in their truth-seeking and hatred of evil in all its forms. In a later age and a different climate of opinion McCrae might have followed Bethune in his search for a society structured so that it would not produce the inequalities which lead to war.

This book is a further reminder that militarism and war are never answers to the dilemmas of the human condition. The solution has been tried many times and has failed consistently. As the world drifts into new forms of militarism and barbarism we need the qualities and courage of men like John McCrae to seek better ways to solve the complex problems which face us.

ABOUT THE AUTHOR

John Prescott was born in Libya to English army parents. He spent his childhood moving from British colony to British colony as they achieved independence. He went to school at Ampleforth in England and graduated from Cambridge (Vet M.B., 1973 and PhD. 1977). Since 1976 he has worked as a veterinary bacteriologist at the Ontario Veterinary College. A recent Canadian, he is married with two young sons. The family lives in Guelph, Ontario.

His background for writing this book includes an interest in First World War poets, in veterinary and medical history, and first-hand knowledge of the army and of the remnants of the British Empire.

BIBLIOGRAPHY

I PRIMARY SOURCES

The following sources were particularly helpful for this book, and are quoted extensively in the footnotes. The abbreviation used for these sources in the footnotes is given in parentheses.

1. Public Archives of Canada. Letters from John McCrae to his parents, especially his mother, from his University of Toronto days to the end of the Boer War; letters to his mother from France 1916-1918; letters to Oskar Klotz. (PAC)
2. McCrae's Birthplace Museum, Guelph, Ontario. John McCrae's childhood and family scrapbooks; the *Daily Mercury* newspaper clippings of John McCrae's description of his Boer War experiences, culled from the letters to his mother; photographs and other artifacts. (MBM)
3. Osler Library, McGill University, Montreal. Much archival and published material on John McCrae and his contemporaries, including letters to Edward Archibald. (OSLER)
4. Macphail, A.: *In Flanders Fields and other poems* by Lt Col John McCrae, with *An Essay in Character* by Sir Andrew Macphail. Toronto: Williams Briggs, 1919. (MACPHAIL)

II SECONDARY SOURCES

Under each chapter heading in the footnotes are given the most relevant of the books used in that chapter. General books on the period which were consulted and books on the poetry of the Great War and on McCrae's contemporaries are listed below. They are referred to in the footnotes by the author's name in capital letters. Dates of publication refer to copies of books available to me.

Berger, C.: *The Sense of Power: Studies in the Ideas of Canadian Imperialism, 1867-1914.* Toronto: Oxford University Press, 1970.
Bergonzi, B.: *Heroes' Twilight.* London: Constable, 1965.
Bowle, J.: *The Imperial Achievement.* London: Pelican, 1977.
Brown, R.C., and R. Cook: *Canada 1896-1921. A Nation Transformed.* Toronto: McClelland and Stewart, 1976.
Fussell, P.: *The Great War and Modern Memory.* Oxford: Oxford University Press, 1975.
Gardner, B.: *Up the Line to Death — The War Poets 1914-1918.* London: Methuen, 1964.
Goodspeed, D.J.: *The Road Past Vimy.* Toronto: Macmillan, 1969.
Johnson, L.A.: *History of Guelph 1827-1927.* Guelph: Guelph Historical Society, 1977.

Johnston, J.H.: *English Poetry of the First World War*. Princeton: Princeton University Press, 1964.

Jones, D.: *In Parenthesis*. London: Faber and Faber, 1937.

Lewis, D.S.: *Royal Victoria Hospital 1887-1947*. Montreal: McGill University Press, 1969.

Liddell Hart, B.H.: *History of the First World War*. London: Pan Books, 1977.

MacDermot, H.E.: *A History of the Montreal General Hospital*. Montreal: Montreal General Hospital, 1950.

Macphail, A.: *In Flanders Fields and Other Poems* by Lt Col John McCrae, with An Essay in Character. Toronto: William Briggs, 1919.

Macphail, A.: *The Medical Services. Official History of the Canadian Forces in the Great War, 1914-1919*. Ottawa: Department of National Defence, 1925.

Mathieson, W.D.: *My Grandfather's War. Canadians Remember the First World War 1914-1918*. Toronto: Macmillan, 1981.

Montague, C.E.: *Disenchantment*. London: MacGibbon and Kee, 1968.

Morrison, E.W.B.: *The War as Morrison Saw It*. Ottawa: Sunday Evening Citizen, 1928.

Mottram, R.H.: *Spanish Farm Trilogy, 1914-1918*. London: Penguin Modern Classics, 1979.

Pakenham, T.: *The Boer War*. New York: Random House, 1979.

Reid, G.: *Poor Bloody Murder — Personal Memoirs of the First World War*. Oakville, Ontario: Mosaic Press, 1980.

Reid, W.S. (ed.): *The Scottish Tradition in Canada*. Toronto: McClelland and Stewart, 1976.

Tuchman, B.: *The Proud Tower. A Portrait of the World Before the War, 1890-1914*. New York: Bantam Books, 1980.

Young, G.M.: *Portrait of an Age: Victorian England*. Oxford: Oxford University Press, 1977.

FOOTNOTES

CHAPTER ONE

Byerly, A.E.: *The McCraes of Guelph.* Elora, Ontario, 1932.

Gow, J.E.: *John Eckford and His Family — Bruce Pioneers.* Quebec, 1911.

McCrae, A.: *The History of the Clan McCrae.* Dingwall: Ross and Co., 1899.

CHAPTER TWO

Ross, A.M.: *The College on the Hill — A History of the Ontario Agricultural College 1874-1974.* Toronto, 1974.

[1] Howitt, H.O.: John McCrae. *McGill Daily News* (no date). MBM.

[2] Letter from W.W. Francis to H.O. Howitt, 1941. OSLER.

[3] Letter from unnamed source to W.W. Francis. OSLER.

[4] This and subsequent quotes from: Report of the Commission of Inquiry as to the Ontario Agricultural College and Experimental Farm. Toronto: Ontario Government, 1893.

CHAPTER THREE

[1] University of Toronto Calendar, 1896-1897.

[2] MACPHAIL.

[3] MACPHAIL.

[4] MACPHAIL.

CHAPTER FOUR

Bernheim, B.M.: *The Story of the Johns Hopkins.* New York: McGraw-Hill, 1948.

Cushing, H.: *The Life of Sir William Osler.* Oxford University Press, 1925.

Reid, E.G.: *The Great Physician — A Short Life of Sir William Osler.* Oxford University Press, 1931.

[1] Thomas McCrae was a close associate and friend of both Osler and his wife, Grace. He worked at Johns Hopkins from 1896 until 1912, when he took the chair of clinical medicine at Jefferson Medical College in Philadelphia. He largely edited *A System of Modern Medicine*, written by Osler and himself, in seven large volumes. John McCrae wrote several chapters for it. Tom McCrae married Osler's niece, Amy Gwyn of Dundas, in 1908.

[2] Cushing.

[3] Reid.

[4] Reid.

[5] Cushing.

[6] Cushing.

[7] TUCHMAN.

[8] TUCHMAN.

[9] TUCHMAN.

CHAPTER FIVE

Morris, J.: *Pax Britannica — The Climax of Empire*. London: Penguin Books, 1979.

Morrison, E.W.B.: *With the Guns in South Africa*. Hamilton, Ontario: Spectator Printing Co., 1901.

[1] BOWLE.

[2] PAKENHAM.

[3] BROWN and COOK.

[4] MACPHAIL.

[5] MBM.

[6] MBM.

[7] John McCrae's Boer War letters to his mother. PAC.

[8] *Ibid.*

[9] *Ibid.*

[10] *Ibid.*

[11] *Ibid.*

[12] MBM.

[13] *Ibid.*

[14] *Ibid.*

[15] *Ibid.*

[16] McCrae, J.: *Builders of Empire*. *University Magazine*.

CHAPTER SIX

Howell, W.B.: *Francis John Shepherd — Surgeon*. Toronto: Dent and Sons, 1934.

MacDermot, H.E.: *Sir Thomas Roddick*. Toronto: Macmillan, 1938.

Shepherd, F.J.: *Origin and History of the Montreal General Hospital*. Montreal: Gazette Printing Co., 1925.

[1] Adami, M. (ed.): *J.G. Adami — A Memoir*. London: Constable, 1930.

[2] *Ibid.*

[3] *Ibid.*

[4] *Ibid.*

[5] MacDermot, H.E.: *Canadian Med Assoc J* 40:495, 1939.

[6] MACPHAIL.

[7] Adami.

[8] Howitt, H.O.: *McGill Daily News* (no date). MBM.

[9] Klotz, O.: *American J Med Sci*, Philadelphia, 1918.

[10] McCrae, J.: *Montreal Med J* 34:32, 1905.

CHAPTER SEVEN

[1] MACPHAIL.

[2] Leacock, S.: Obituary of John McCrae. London *Times*, 1921. MBM.

[3] MACPHAIL.

[4] McCrae, J.: *Maritime Med Assoc News* (no date). OSLER.

[5] McCrae, J.: *Montreal Med J* 37:627, 1908.

6 McCrae, J.: *Montreal Med J* 38:523, 1909.
7 Klotz, Oskar - John McCrae Letters. PAC.
8 MacDermot, H.E.: Dr. Edward Archibald. Obituary in unknown journal. OSLER.
9 MACPHAIL.
10 Leacock, S.: *op. cit.*

CHAPTER EIGHT
Amery, L.S.: *Days of Fresh Air*. London: Jarrolds, 1939.
1 BERGER.
2 BERGER.
3 BERGER.
4 MBM.
5 Leacock, S.: Sir Andrew Macphail. Obituary in untraceable source.
6 Macnaughton, J.: In Memoriam - Lt Col John McCrae. *University Magazine*. 1918.
7 MACPHAIL.
8 Amery.
9 Begbie, H.: *Albert, 4th Earl Grey. A Last Word*. Toronto: Hodder and Stoughton, 1917. (Quoted by kind permission of the publishers.)
10 *Ibid*.
11 *Ibid*.
12 PAKENHAM.
13 Begbie.
14 *Ibid*.
15 Amery. L.S.: *My Political Life*. Volume 1. London: Hutchinson, 1953.
16 *Ibid*.

CHAPTER NINE
1 Lewis, D.S.: Montreal *Gazette*, November 1978.
2 Klotz, Oskar - John McCrae Letters. PAC.
3 Lewis.
4 Klotz, Oscar - John McCrae Letters. PAC.
5 *Ibid*.
6 Macnaughton, J.: *op cit* chapter 8.
7 MACPHAIL.
8 MACPHAIL.
9 MACPHAIL.

CHAPTER TEN
Boyd, W.: *With a Field Ambulance at Ypres*. Toronto: Musson, 1916.
Nasmith, G.: *On the Fringe of the Great Fight*. Toronto: McClelland, Goodchild, and Stewart, 1917.
1 Dangerfield, G.: *The Strange Death of Liberal England, 1910-1914*. New York: Capricorn Books, 1961.

141

2   Macphail, A.: *Canadian Med Assoc J* 4:803, 1914.
3   MACPHAIL.
4   MBM.
5   MORRISON.
6   *Ibid.*
7   Allinson, C.L.C.: John McCrae - Poet, Soldier, Physician. Unpublished manuscript. (Quoted by kind permission of Mrs. Cynthia McLeod.)
8   Cushing, *op cit.* Chapter 4.
9   Nasmith.
10 Currie, J.A.: *The Red Watch. With the First Canadian Division in Flanders.* Toronto: McClelland, Goodchild, and Stewart, 1916.
11 C.F. Martin - John McCrae Letters. (Quoted by kind permission of Mrs. R. Gardner-Medwin and the Royal College of Physicians and Surgeons of Canada.)
12 MACPHAIL.
13 Letter from W.W. Francis to H.O. Howitt, 1941. OSLER.
14 Allinson.

CHAPTER ELEVEN
Aitken, M.: *Canada in Flanders.* London: Hodder and Stoughton, 1916.
Allen, R.: *Ordeal by Fire.* Toronto: Popular Library, 1961.
1   MACPHAIL. (Unless otherwise noted all quotes in this chapter are from the letters printed in MACPHAIL.)
2   MORRISON.
3   *Ibid.*
4   Letter to Billy (Turner?) from McCrae. (Quoted with permission of Mrs. R. Gardner Medwin and the Guelph Public Library.)
5   C.F. Martin - John McCrae Letters, *op cit.* Chapter 10.
6   LIDDELL HART.
7   Allinson, *op cit.* Chapter 10.
8   Letter to Billy (Turner?).
9   Allinson.
10 *Ibid.*
11 MBM.
12 MACPHAIL.
13 Allinson.
14 The unprecedented torpedoeing, with great loss of life, of the unarmed passenger liner *Lusitania* made a sensation around the world. Together with the German use of poison gas it did much to awaken the British to the seriousness of the German threat.
15 Allinson.
16 Cushing, *op cit.* Chapter 4.

CHAPTER TWELVE
Fetherstonhaugh, R.C.: *Number 3 Canadian General Hospital (McGill),* *1914-1919.* Montreal: Gazette Publishing Co.

[1] Letter from Dr Edward Archibald to his wife, August 1915. OSLER.

[2] *Ibid.*

[3] Howard, A.C.P.: *Sir William Osler Memorial Volume*. Montreal: *Bull. Intern Assoc. Med Museums*, 1926.

[4] Letter from Sir William Osler to Marjorie Futcher, March 1916. Quoted from R. Palmer Howard, *The Chief - Dr William Osler*. Canton, Mass.: Watson Publishing International, 1983. (Quoted with kind permission of Dr R. Palmer Howard.)

[5] Cushing, *op cit*. Chapter 4.

[6] *Ibid.*

[7] Maurois, A.: *The Life of Sir Alexander Fleming*. London: Jonathan Cape, 1959.

[8] MACPHAIL.

[9] Leacock, *op cit*. Chapter 7.

[10] Letter from John McCrae to his mother in 1916-1918 correspondence in PAC.

[11] *Ibid.*

[12] *The Herald* had opposed the establishment of a railway junction in Guelph; David McCrae had been a director of the company which promoted it.

CHAPTER THIRTEEN

Watson, F.: *Dawson of Penn*. London: Chatto and Windus, 1950.

Wilkinson, A.: *The Church of England and the First World War*. London: Society for the Propagation of the Christian Faith, 1978.

Wolff, L.: *In Flanders Fields. The 1917 Campaign*. London: Penguin Books, 1977.

[1] MACPHAIL.

[2] Adami, J.G.: *British Med J*, 1918.

[3] Letters from McCrae to his mother, 1916-1918, unless otherwise indicated all quotes in this chapter are from these letters. PAC.

[4] Letter from Lady Osler to Harvey Cushing, January 1918. OSLER.

[5] Letter from Lady Osler to T.A. Malloch, 1918. OSLER.

[6] Fetherstonhaugh, *op cit*. Chapter 12.

[7] FUSSELL.

[8] MONTAGUE.

[9] *Ibid.*

[10] *Ibid.*

[11] MOTTRAM.

[12] MBM.

[13] Cushing, *op cit*. Chapter 4.

[14] Letter from McCrae to Dr Edward Archibald, October 1917. OSLER.

[15] Cushing, H.: *From a Surgeon's Journal, 1915-1918*. London: Constable, 1936.

[16] Fetherstonhaugh.

17 Letter from Margaret Woods to Miss Hall. PAC.

18 Elder, J.M.: *British Med J*, 1918.

19 Letter in Victoria *Times*, by Carleton Hannington: quoted in MATHIESON. Reprinted from the *Daily Colonist* of 15 Dec., 1918, courtesy of the *Times-Colonist*, Victoria, B.C.

CHAPTER FOURTEEN

1 Macphail, A.: In Retrospect — Armistice Day 1936. Manuscript in PAC, source unknown.